Cocker Hoop

LES COCKER
The Biography

Cocker Hoop
Key Man for Ramsey and Revie

Robert Endeacott and Dave Cocker

First published by Pitch Publishing, 2022

Pitch Publishing
9 Donnington Park,
85 Birdham Road,
Chichester,
West Sussex,
PO20 7AJ
www.pitchpublishing.co.uk
info@pitchpublishing.co.uk

© 2022, Robert Endeacott and Dave Cocker

Every effort has been made to trace the copyright.
Any oversight will be rectified in future editions at the
earliest opportunity by the publisher.

All rights reserved. No part of this book may be reproduced,
sold or utilised in any form or transmitted in any form or by
any means, electronic or mechanical, including photocopying,
recording or by any information storage and retrieval system,
without prior permission in writing from the Publisher.

A CIP catalogue record is available for this book
from the British Library.

ISBN 978 1 80150 147 7

Typesetting and origination by Pitch Publishing
Printed and bound in Great Britain by TJ Books, Padstow

Contents

Foreword	11
Introduction	14
1. The beginning	17
2. World War Two to 1959	23
3. Leeds and England dreaming	55
4. 1965 – on the up	88
5. 1966, England's glory	99
6. 1967 to 1970 – Leeds' time and turn for glory?	123
7. 1970 – Mexico and after	161
8. 1972 – t'FA Cup	172
9. 1974 and past it?	198
10. Two eras	209
11. The UAE and then 'Donny'	233
Epilogue	245
Acknowledgements and Thanks	249
Bibliography	252

'cock-a-hoop'

adjective

extremely and obviously pleased, especially about an achievement

Dedicated to Les and Nora Cocker, and all their family and friends

Foreword

I WAS very pleased to be invited by Robert and Dave to provide the foreword for this biography of Les Cocker, a colleague for over a decade. Les and I enjoyed a good working relationship throughout and I'm looking forward to reading the book once it's finished. I'm sure it will be a really interesting read about a fine man who deserved all the accolades he has received.

I didn't really know much about Les in the early days of my playing career, which was starting while his was coming to a close. Following his years as a player, his new role would be in coaching which involved much more than just the learning of formations and tactics.

When I joined Leeds United from FA Cup holders Manchester United in August 1963, some people probably doubted my judgement, if not my sanity, as Leeds were in the Second Division at the time. I could have easily answered those doubters by saying that it was all part of my big plan and that I knew exactly what I was doing, but of course there is always doubt in a player's mind when they're changing football clubs, whatever era we're talking about. In my case, though, the move wasn't as impulsive as it might have seemed; I'd been watching Leeds' situation with interest and was sure that they were going places, so when Don Revie came in to sign me, it didn't take much persuasion. He made it clear to me that I would be a big part of his plans for the future of the club, and that would start immediately with a full-on push for promotion to the First Division. It was definitely the right time for me to change clubs. Les was already at the club, as was Syd Owen who had been a great player (and Footballer of the Year in 1959) and would prove to be a great influence and asset, so it was clear Leeds meant real business.

A big influence on my decision was, without a doubt, the presence of Bobby Collins at Elland Road. The signing of Bobby had been huge. At the time, Leeds were struggling in the lower half of the Second Division while Scottish international Bobby was at First Division Everton. You couldn't get a better example than Bobby of how to play and how to be a good professional. Everyone in the game was aware of his quality, not only as a player but for his leadership, professionalism, his competitive edge and his will to win, so for Don and Harry Reynolds to get him to play for Leeds was a real coup and statement of intent. They were developing a fine squad of players and had very good coaching and training personnel, men who knew what they were doing and knew what they wanted to achieve because the whole club was united in its ambition. Les Cocker was certainly one of those men;

he was crucial and integral for Leeds United's improvement and growth.

Les's honesty, integrity and willingness to help anyone were always plain to see, and his influence and positive effect on the players and the club as a whole cannot be underestimated. Everyone associated with the club knew they could trust him, rely on him and learn from him. Time and time again he proved himself to be an outstanding coach, trainer and even physio. His contribution to the cause of Leeds United *and* England should never be overlooked or allowed to be forgotten, and I hope and trust that this book will help to reinforce that feeling.

Best wishes

John Giles

Les Cocker, John Giles and Billy Bremner

Introduction

WHENEVER I have mentioned that this biography was happening, a frequent response has been, 'It's about time!', along with how much Les Cocker's story deserves telling. He has, for me and, I suspect, many more football supporters, been one of those figures frequently seen in league and international football – especially 1966 – who very little has been reported on.

A certain film which, for the purposes of this book I shall call *Carry On Clough* – with no disrespect towards the fabulously inappropriate *Carry On* series – depicts Les as some sort of callous, dishonest bully. I try to be objective and reasonable in my ways but have to say, what a load of codswallop that film is. He is not the only one badly characterised in the film, of course; it is quite disgraceful in spite of a couple of excellent performances. Anyway, dear reader, you will see here that in reality he was a good and caring and dedicated man, a consummate professional who gave everything his best shot and who would readily help anyone in need. He needed to be resilient in his work but the simple fact is, that his intentions were to help achieve the best results for everyone he worked with. If he coached 'you' then it was you who he wanted to benefit, not himself, to help you realise your ambitions and be the best you could be in your field.

Throughout my reading and research of numerous articles, biographies and autobiographies for this book, I've been intrigued by how many themes, events and attributes resonate with and sternly link prominent characters in Les's story. Revie and Ramsey for example, considered by many to be polar opposites, shared similarly strong views on certain matters, mainly football related of course. And a faithful yet independently minded lieutenant for both was, of course, Les Cocker.

I'm extremely grateful to the interviewees for their contributions to this book, and I know many of you will understand what a personal thrill it has always been to speak with famous figures, heroes even, of my childhood. Unfortunately, I didn't manage to collar all of my targets; Mr Keegan is a difficult man to get hold of and I must have followed the wrong yellow brick road in trying to reach Sir Elton John!

One thing I've learnt in life from favourite forefathers is that your best efforts are the minimum requirement, the very least you should give, whatever your task. For various reasons that we all have been affected by, *Cocker Hoop* has been at times difficult to proceed with but it has always been a rewarding journey, thanks mainly to Les's family, friends and colleagues for their help and goodwill. Although I never properly met him

– I'm not sure I even got his autograph – I grew up 'knowing' him and his achievements with Leeds and, of course, England. A story my parents told me about him made me understand what a fine chap he was. On the official Leeds United train journey home after the 1972 FA Cup Final, with my dad Barry and mum Moyra on board thanks to Dad being on the ground staff at Elland Road, the FA Cup – filled with champagne – was shared around among the lucky occupants of the train carriages in celebration. It's a long time ago, of course, but I think I'm right in saying that it was the first time Mum ever drank champagne. Anyway, this gesture was instigated by Les who, perhaps surprisingly, was on board along with Don Revie. Coincidentally, Les's eldest son, Dave, was also there, and you can read of his exploits then and on other occasions later on.

Thank you for investing in this book. I hope you enjoy reading it even half as much as I did researching and writing it.

Robert Endeacott, March 2022

PS Thank you, Marcelo Bielsa, for bringing Leeds United back to life. Your wisdom, dignity and football doctrine will always be remembered and never allowed to be forgotten.

1

The beginning

WITHOUT WISHING to reveal any major plot spoilers of Les Cocker's story, here are a couple of quotes I unearthed about him. For me, they perfectly encapsulate aspects of the man's character.

The first comes from an Accrington Stanley match programme of 1954, when Les was aged 30 and a 'seasoned' attacker for 'The Owd Reds': 'Les Cocker is now in his second season at the club and has proved a great servant with a heart to match his ability. He is a nuisance, he never lets an opponent settle and he can snatch goals in brilliant style.'

Though Les was at Leeds at the time, the second quote comes from an Aldershot versus Stockport programme in the early 1970s, referring to his playing days: 'It's difficult to remember anyone who grafted for 90 minutes as much as he did. Courage and determination were his answer to his lack of inches.'

You will see in this book that all of these Cocker qualities remained as constants throughout his life and that he shared common bonds and characteristics with many other football men of the same era. Hardship, war and conscription undoubtedly helped to unite those of a certain age, and we owe much to Les's generation in helping to rebuild the country and enabling football to thrive in spite of all the huge obstacles.

Les was born on 13 March 1924, in Stockport. Curiously enough, Fred Perry was also born there, 15 years earlier, though the acclaimed tennis icon has nothing else to do with this book. And besides, Perry was moved away to Bolton and, later, Wallasey, by his parents when he was but a nipper. Artist Laurence Stephen Lowry created some of his wonderful paintings and drawings in Stockport, famously reproducing images of the town including, in the 1950s, the renowned Stockport viaduct which supposedly used 11 million bricks in its construction; it was at the time of its completion, in 1840, the largest viaduct in the world. The town also possesses the Stockport Plaza, a beautiful example of 1930s Art Deco architecture. Stockport would share some of the music limelight thanks to the formation of Strawberry Studios in the late 1960s, above the Nield and Hardy record store and ostensibly owned by a fledgling band called 10cc. In later years, Paul McCartney, Joy Division and the Stone Roses would record there.

Geographically, most of Stockport lay within the boundaries of the county of Cheshire, though its land north of the River Mersey was classified as Lancashire. Also news to me is that, in Stockport, the confluence of two rivers – the

THE BEGINNING

Goyt and the Tame – form the famous Mersey. Since the 17th century, a main industry in the town was hat-making, and it employed a significant percentage of the local population, with over six million hats a year exported. Hence Stockport County Football Club, formed in 1883 (as Heaton Norris Rovers at the time), were nicknamed the Hatters.

Even with the constant horrors we are witnessing in today's world, I can't help but think that life felt tougher in the 1920s for most Britons, primarily due to fewer social and economic avenues of help. What life was like for a child like Les, in working-class society still overcast by silver lining-less clouds of a world war, feels too obscure, too distant a picture to realistically visualise. Was it even possible for a 1920s family to have a happy life in a small, north-west industrial town? And if the direct consequences of World War One weren't enough to contend with, the Great Depression would hit home by the decade's end.

The emphasis on a good upbringing generally rests with family, and Les's parents as well as his two sisters, Dorothy and Jessie, undoubtedly helped build a settled, secure and, I dare say, content life. With a spirit of stoicism typical of probably every region in Britain at the time, in those pre-NHS times and with acutely less awareness of mental health issues, it was considered that people ought to just 'get on with it' and 'take the rough with the smooth' even if the smooth seemed an alien prospect.

Stockport was a place of many terraced houses and cobbled streets – all very *Coronation Street*-ish, if you will, which is not surprising as Corrie was originally, and still is, set in nearby Manchester ('Weatherfield', to be more accurate). The Cocker family home was respectable, appealing, clean, reasonably warm and 'nothing fancy' – just what a working-class home should be. Manchester is notorious for its rainy weather, but that's a rich comment coming from me, in Leeds, as I've just checked the rainfall stats for my home town. Anyway, life in the 1920s and 30s will have felt permanently gloomy and overcast for many British people in the wake of World War One and the ongoing, deeply worrying political rumbles in Europe. The nation needed that high degree of stoicism, I feel, to face up to general life and to be prepared for hard times ahead. How this affected the general demeanour and outlooks of children in such a climate is open to question, but it's a common belief that they grew up to be resilient, intuitive, independent and pragmatic.

There certainly was a baby boom after the war and generational life expectancy always improves as the years and societies progress. Those were the days when strong community spirit was vital, with family, friends and neighbours helping each other out in times of need. Of which there were many. The age-old theory applied, that households were able to happily leave their doors unlocked as the times were more innocent and neighbourly. Myself, I've always suspected that the happiest and least worried members of society in such times were the burglars of Great Britain.

THE BEGINNING

Like a slow-burn virus, the Great Depression hit the United States following the Wall Street Crash of 1929, sending economic and social shockwaves around the world. For Britain and Europe the consequences were wide-ranging, thanks in part to the demand from the US for exports declining, resulting in large-scale unemployment in many countries.. Here, the number of unemployed rose in to the millions and soup kitchens became commonplace around the country. Government reports declared that around a quarter of the British population were 'barely existing' on a poor subsistence diet. Child malnutrition increased and this blight in turn resulted in a disturbing rise in cases of scurvy, rickets – due to vitamin deficiencies – and tuberculosis. Tuberculosis was particularly serious, a killer disease with no widespread vaccinations against it available. 'TB' would only begin to be dealt with proficiently in the 1950s, a few years after the National Health Service had been created in 1948.

Hard, grey times indeed, creating and reinforcing the need for football escapism on a Saturday afternoon for swathes of men around Great Britain. The sport was a cheaper form of both realism and romanticism than cinema, delivering genuine human bonding, brotherhood, hope, drama and heroes to the fore. The terraces were often packed with Mackintosh raincoats, ties, trilby hats, pipes, four-page matchday programmes, Bovril and gravy-stuffed pies to scorch the mouth. There is no surprise that today there is a yearning for these days of innocent wonder; it was a beautiful thing amidst the hardships that were endured by so many. We, the people, were the roses growing and blooming through the pavement cracks of tough working-class towns. The likes of Stockport and Accrington were represented as tough and dour football clubs. A not too unkind summary, though both were staunch pillars of local community life. Others, such as Luton Town and Leeds United, were higher in status but, in reality not much better off.

Football was never just a game; it was important, it was significant, it was a low-cost high-value pastime, a frequently glorious pastime bringing colour to many a grey life. The young Les Cocker appreciated this, and if he wasn't playing football in the street, then it was more than likely he was playing cricket instead, and all that before the other sporting obsession of his life, golf. You probably know already, that Les would 'make it' in football, but he was also a fine cricketer, even better with the bat and ball than he was with the golf club and dimpled projectile.

2

World War Two to 1959

LES COCKER lived with his parents and sisters in Regent Road in Heaviley, not two miles away from Stockport County's Edgeley Park stadium. On leaving school at 15, his chosen trade was as a painter and decorator, but his first love was football and his dream was to be a professional player. His father, Frank Cocker, had served in World War One and had, like many other men in wartime, including professional footballers, played in overseas tournaments organised by the army. It was good for personal fitness and it was good for the men's morale. A winner's medal awarded to him shows that his team were actually successful in one of these tournaments. Back home after the war, Frank ran a number of local teams for several years, knowing the value of sport in community. There was minimal chance of Les *not* getting involved; it was clearly in his blood from the earliest of ages.

At the age of 13 he had played regularly for his Cale Green School side and also represented Stockport Boys in 1938. Early in September 1939, with World War Two recently commenced, the Football Association ruled that all football except that organised by the armed forces was suspended until further official notice. Various reasons were cited for this, including the threat of German air attacks on crowded locations, plus the introduction of a new National Service Act: conscription for 18- to 41-year-old men living in Great Britain. However, later that month the Home Office agreed to allow limited regional league and cup fixtures providing they did not interfere with national service and industry. Football was, after all, good for public morale too, even though the match attendances were limited during wartime.

By 1941 and with the war raging on, Les, now the required age, was called on to complete his six months' national service training; this took place at Catterick, North Yorkshire. Once that was finished, he was transferred to the other end of the country, the south coast, to be stationed at the Lulworth army base in Dorset. He was now a member of the Reconnaissance Regiment of the 53rd Division – also known as the 'Recce Battalion' or corps – formed during World War Two to provide reconnaissance for the British army's infantry divisions.

His regiment went to France in 1944 and on D-Day, 6 June, Les suffered a head injury during combat. It was an incident he rarely spoke of afterwards – indeed, he was generally reticent about his involvement and the war – and so the personal details and experiences always remained vague. To officially confirm his injury, a medical postcard was delivered by the army to

Les's parents, with 'On his majesty's service – Advice of Admission to Hospital' printed on the front. The details on the reverse were just as helpful, the stamped line declaring 'NOT NECESSARY TO VISIT AT PRESENT' underneath, which was the handwritten comment of 'Head' next to the printed subtitle of 'Wounded'. Imagine how much comfort the Cocker family was able to take from such a considerate and compassionate missive!

In later years, Les's only comment to his family about the wound would be that it was 'just a graze'. Such a statement was typical for the day and of young men who had personally witnessed too many appalling sights during their times in combat. Les never appreciated a 'fuss' over himself anyway, also a common characteristic of the era, but to describe any head injury needing hospital treatment as 'just a graze' suggests an underestimation of the situation, as well as of the shock it undoubtedly caused at home.

The postcard came via the hospital treating him, St Hugh's College Hospital in Oxford, which at its peak of the Normandy campaign of 1944 provided 430 beds for the treatment of service personnel. Between 1940 and 1945, around 13,000 patients in all had been referred to St Hugh's where 'groundbreaking research into the management of head injuries' had been conducted.

World War Two stretched from September 1939 to September 1945 in Europe, and Football League games were cancelled for the duration. The restrictions on matches continued for around a year. During that time, professional footballers regularly made guest appearances for teams – though not of their personal choice; instead they were 'assigned' to clubs by the army. Les apparently played once for Arsenal, and also a few times in the same side as Tom Finney, two years older. There are claims too that Les appeared for Darlington, Brighton and, on one occasion, Leeds, but records to substantiate this have so far proved elusive. Although based in Dorset, Les sometimes was assigned to appear in matches in the north, not too far from home, but wasn't allowed to visit home, regardless of how close it was to the match venue. Once the final whistle had been blown, players in the forces were under strict instruction to return to base as soon as was possible.

In 1942, Les played as a wartime guest for Manvers Main in the final of the Montagu Cup against Upton Colliery, and, as an outside-right, scored a hat-trick in the 4-2 win. The final was staged at Denaby United, with gate takings a 'disappointing' £23. It was Manvers Main's third consecutive cup win. Manvers Main's publicity stated that Les at the time was on Arsenal's books.

His officially acknowledged involvement with professional football began in unusual circumstances, and that is really saying something considering the era. On Saturday, 6 October 1945, he was home on leave from Dorset and had decided to travel to watch his team (Stockport County, naturally) play away against Accrington Stanley in Division Three (North

West) of the War League. He travelled to the Peel Park stadium as a spectator but, with County apparently short of a full 11, the 'unknown' (as the *Stockport Advertiser* described him) Les Cocker was brought into the side as left-half. Possessing 'good ball control and delivery' and knowing 'how to keep his body between the ball and the opponent', his reputation as a more-than-decent player seemed to have preceded him. Sadly, the match proved to be less 'Roy of the Rovers' and more 'Cocker of the County' stuff, with Accrington winning 3-0. That said, Les must have done something right in the match as, within weeks, he signed professional terms for the club.

On 8 December, a sign of his versatility came with his selection in the position of left-back. He played well in the 2-0 win over Chester, though it was said that a substantial part of the reason for this was that he had been helped by the broader experience and know-how of guest player 'F. Williams' from Southampton. Regardless of the match results and the quality of Les's performances, a testament of his dedication to the game, and to County, was that for every fixture he had to make a round trip of around 250 miles from his army base in Dorset. Of course, that is not just a sign of his dedication, it also shows a love for the game.

After the war had ended, Les indirectly made it into the newspapers, although it wasn't exactly a claim to fame. On 30 March 1946 Stockport County hosted Doncaster Rovers in the second leg of a Division Three (North) Cup match. The first game had finished 2-2, and the return leg resulted in the same scoreline, so extra time was played. With no further goals scored, and no set rule about the duration of extra time (it was, effectively, 'next goal wins'), the game went on and on. After a little under three hours of play, Les turned the ball into the Doncaster net and the crowd, reportedly, went wild and some spectators even invaded the pitch to congratulate the hero. But then the referee blew his whistle for an infringement; he had spotted a handball and so disallowed the goal. The match continued, and soon players were 'collapsing with exhaustion' while the crowd, who can't have been too energetic either by that time, implored the referee to call it a day. Finally, in the dusk and with a haze of smoke from the nearby railway hanging over the ground, the referee decided that the light was too poor to continue. All in all, the match had lasted 203 minutes. A last replay took place a few days later, which Doncaster won 4-0.

For the 1946/47 season, the Football League returned to its pre-war format of First Division, Second Division, Third Division (North) and Third Division (South). There is not an abundance of material relating to Les's playing career, nor, with respect, were Stockport likely to be newspaper headline-makers, but it is clear that club and Cocker were well-suited: honest, gritty, hard-working. He was never what could be called the most refined of performers, yet the positives of his ability easily outweighed the negatives: tenacious, eager to please, hungry and always ready for combat, in the most sporting of senses. A report from late January 1947 seemed to typify his robust approach to playing, confirming that he had been unable to return to barracks after an injury suffered in the first half of the Saturday, 25 January 2-0 home win over Barrow. He had suffered a badly bruised ankle after crashing into the Railway End railings of the stadium – almost guaranteed to be after he had chased a seemingly lost cause – and had been confined to bed at home as a consequence. The accident probably got him into bother back at his army base, too, as his full recovery took more than a fortnight and he was only able to return there on 13 February 1947.

His first honours came in one of the county of Cheshire's cup competitions. Two separate events were staged each season – the Cheshire Senior Cup, open to league and non-league teams in the region, and the Cheshire Bowl which was open to full Football League sides only. Stockport won the 1947 Senior Cup through a 1-0 victory over Hyde United. In the Third Division (North), Stockport finished fourth place out of 24 teams, having earned 50 points, 22 fewer than champions Doncaster Rovers. Les had played in 21 league games and scored nine goals, a not-too-poor effort by any measure. He also appeared in four FA Cup games, scoring once.

The following season was a disappointment. Stockport finished 17th, on 28 points, while Les completed just 11 league games, scoring one goal, and one FA Cup game with no goals scored. There was to be, though, an exciting new signing for the new season, with Alec Herd arriving from Manchester City. Probably not a particularly memorable name nowadays but it was big news for the town at that time. Herd, although in his 37th year, was a Scottish inside-forward who undoubtedly could still 'cut the mustard'. He joined on a free transfer from Manchester City where he had scored 107 goals in 257 league games and won the FA Cup and the First Division title during the 1930s.

During the Cheshire Senior Cup semi-final in March 1949 at Hyde, Les needed hospital treatment due to a back injury suffered in extra time. No doubt the pain will have been eased a little by the knowledge that Stockport were victorious. The hospital discharged him on the following Monday, and the team later went on to win the cup, beating Winsford United 2-0 in the final, after extra time. The match was staged at Crewe Alexandra's Gresty Road ground on 16 April 1949, and over 10,000 attended. Reports said Winsford performed well and could count themselves perhaps unfortunate to have not taken an early lead. In the end though, Stockport's superior fitness helped them take the trophy, with most of the attacking play coming from the professional team. Les played and, naturally, never stopped grafting, though he missed a decent chance in the second half, overrunning the ball when through on goal.

Perhaps even better, they also triumphed in the Cheshire Bowl, beating Tranmere Rovers 2-1, after extra time, in the final at Edgeley Park. It had been a dour contest and the quality of football a disappointment, even with odd spates of ironic cheering from the crowd when one Herd shot soared out of the stadium, followed not long after by a stray corner. Now, whether or not the cup wins made the back-page headlines around the country is quite unimportant, the fact is that the brace was a welcome 'double' for the club. Whatever the level a football team plays in, their targets are always similar: to finish top of the division and to win as many cup matches as they possibly can. Therefore, in all seriousness, two trophy wins in one season equals great success. In the Third Division (North) meanwhile, the team finished eighth with 43 points, although Les appeared in just seven league games and scored once.

The double trophy-winning exploits of 1949 helped to solidly set up the team's next campaign and they hit the ground running, so to speak, from the beginning. The 1949/50 season was certainly the best Stockport enjoyed with Les integrally involved. He played more and scored more, and the team attracted plenty of attention. During the campaign, Doncaster's match programme in January 1950 told readers, 'Les Cocker always harasses the defence and never gives up. Les Cocker is one of the most improved players in the country, lion-hearted, fast and an opportunist.' Such praise in opponents' publications was always a good indication of how highly regarded a player was, even if that player was not a household name around the country. Having said that, Donny won 3-0 so maybe their generous comments had been part of a cunning soft-soaping ploy. Away from the league, Stockport enjoyed a fine FA Cup tournament this season, possibly their best ever, and Les certainly contributed to their impressive efforts.

Their 1949/50 FA Cup quest started in the first round proper, when teams from both regional Third Divisions joined the 25 non-league clubs who had progressed through the qualifying rounds. Stockport were drawn at home to poetically named non-leaguers Billingham Synthonia, 'The Synners'. Research into the name contradicts the suggestion of sweet-scented poeticism, with 'synthonia' being short for synthetic ammonia. Billingham were affiliated with chemicals giant ICI.

This would not be an easy tie for hosts Stockport, despite sitting admirably near the top of their league table. Billingham were renowned battlers and were themselves riding high, second in the Northern League, and would bring hundreds of vociferous supporters with them. Nevertheless, the Stockport team was well prepared and motivated for the match, added impetus always occurring thanks to the anticipation of a home FA Cup tie, regardless of the opposition. In the end, Stockport, in their customary white shirts, worked hard and were well-rewarded with their 3-0 win over the green-and-white-quarter-shirted Billingham. It had been a captivating cup tie.

The draw for the second round proper presented Stockport with, ostensibly, a tougher challenge: Nottingham Forest away. The press predicted a straightforward win for the Third Division (South) team, though the reasons for that were never really made clear. Forest's manager, Billy Walker, was delighted with the draw but also more respectful than the 'experts' concerning Stockport, 'They play some very good football and I think we should stage a very good game. I think this is an obstacle we can surmount but I am always a little chary at making prophecies on cup games.'

Stockport were backed by over 2,000 travelling fans, and morning snowfall had made the City Ground pitch heavy. The visitors appeared to adapt to the conditions more readily and it took just four minutes for Stockport to take the lead, Jimmy McGuigan striking high into the net. The early advantage gave them the perfect fillip and their defence stood strong against whatever Forest could muster. The tie was to be decided with a second goal, on 29 minutes, from 'mastermind' Alec Herd's header from a McGuigan corner. Les Cocker had played his typical style of game, non-stop pressing and harassing of opposing defenders, and he could easily have added to the scoreline had it not been for a couple of timely interceptions and clearances. The 2-0 win was a fair reflection on the match, the better team had won on the day. Cup fever was even rifer in Stockport now, though the rest of English football was yet to be really alerted to the presence of the sole Cheshire team still in the hat.

FA Cup third round ties, even the cup draw itself, perennially generated huge interest and excitement around the football-mad nation. It still possesses the power to do that of course, but to lesser extent thanks to the FA under-valuing the greatest club competition in the world like a golden goose owner promoting the bird as a decent omelette maker. Then, as now, the third round saw the 'big boys' of Division One and Division Two enter the fray. The ties would be played on 7 January 1950 and Stockport had been drawn at home to Second Division Barnsley. The FA Cup was the only nationally contested cup competition in England, a prestigious event which attracted larger crowds than the majority of the clubs' league games. Eternally adding to the appeal of the FA Cup has always been when a lower-league club is paired against a club from a higher level, suggesting a potential giant-killing is in the offing. Barnsley were hardly giants in that respect but they were big enough, and to beat them would, nonetheless, be some achievement by the Hatters, plus the County coffers would benefit.

Beat them they did, 4-2, with Les scoring twice and causing frequent distress to the Barnsley defence with his customary irrepressibility and passion. Defenders hated facing him. In another capacity crowd for Stockport, Barnsley were well supported by over 3,000 of their own fans, many equipped with rattles to increase the noise. It was a lively affair, with both teams looking to attack at every practical opportunity. As was usual for the Stockport side, Herd received most of the plaudits after the match, he being the mastermind and 'schemer', but Les could easily have had a hat-trick in the match. He opened the scoring on five minutes from close range after exploiting dithering defending in the Barnsley back line. However, the visitors equalised 13 minutes later, deservedly, and then looked the likelier of the two teams to win. But Barnsley's defenders then conceded another slack goal, to Swinscoe, in the 27th minute, to spoil the hard work of their colleagues, and it was

2-1 at half-time. The second half continued to be a tight affair but poor defending yet again pretty much decided the outcome, Les seizing on a weak back-pass to Barnsley keeper Hough and slamming the ball home in the 70th minute to make it 3-1. Les had a goal disallowed for handball minutes later, and the visitors scored their second three minutes before time. The drama wasn't over as the next minute saw Les brought down by Hough and a penalty awarded to Stockport. McGuigan scored it and the final score was 4-2.

The fourth round delivered another home tie for Stockport, naturally pleasing the club's directors no end. This time the visitors would be Hull City, strong favourites thanks in part to their present standing of second in the Second Division but also because of the presence in their side of two star names: player-assistant manager Raich Carter and recent £19,000 signing Don Revie. Carter was 36 and in the twilight of his playing career but a footballer of his calibre still had plenty to offer, and Revie was a highly exciting prospect in attack.

On Saturday, 28 January 1950, Hull had two over 2,000 supporters at Edgeley Park, many wearing black and amber scarves and hats (and their mascot was in attendance too, a large figurine tiger) in the official match attendance of 26,600, generating gate receipts of £2,658. Queues had formed since 11am waiting for the turnstiles to open for the 3pm kick-off, while ticket touts were in action also, charging at least double face value for tickets. It was also reported that fans from Barnsley and Nottingham Forest attended.

Alec Herd was outstanding for Stockport, but unfortunately for him so too was Hull goalkeeper Bly. Unsurprisingly, Carter played well for the visitors but it was, overall, a moderate, evenly matched contest, played out on a hard surface in glaring winter sunshine and cold and gusty conditions. Revie tried hard to pierce the Stockport back line but, for most of the match, he and Carter were unable to outwit the close marking and quick tackling of Stockport's backs. Meanwhile, Les made a few dangerous thrusts through the centre without making much headway. The tie stayed goalless.

The replay was quickly scheduled for the afternoon of the following Thursday, 2 February, with tickets printed and on sale on the Monday morning. Stockport would be well supported by their followers, with all their allocation of 900 seats selling out, together with many standing tickets. Come the day, a surprise omission from the Hull line-up gave Stockport even more encouragement – not that they really needed any – with Revie 'rested'. Was that complacency on City's part? We will never know but there was a definite sense that Hull felt they had done the hard work in the drawn match, and that they regarded the replay to be a foregone conclusion. The Stockport players were determined to spring a surprise and they were the dominant, more adventurous side straight from the kick-off. A side of the quality of Hull had their moments but Stockport always looked much the likelier victors. Match reports said Les missed an open goal in the first half, and was also the culprit for a disallowed goal due to being offside (though the referee was probably the only person in attendance to think he had interfered with play). Both incidents, one would imagine, could have haunted him but any such worries were calmed when the oldest player on the pitch, Alec Herd, scored the opener on 33 minutes. It was no more than the underdogs deserved.

The second half continued to be a tough battle, no quarter asked and none given, but a beautiful shot on 68 minutes from Les sealed the win, erasing any of the aforementioned possible concerns and, naturally, galvanising his team even more. Thus it was 2-0 to Stockport and that's how it stayed, signifying a superb and famous win for the Hatters.

The fifth-round draw was made, pairing Stockport with Liverpool, whose boss George Kay was to tell the local media, 'We are satisfied with the draw. We have seen what these supposed minnows of the game can do to the big-wigs of soccer. One has got to forget league status where cup ties are concerned … the cup is something different. It brings clubs much closer together than league games. It is a glorious gamble.' There was probably no one in the football world outside of Stockport who thought County had a chance of winning through to the quarter-finals against the 'mighty' Reds.

The fifth-round ties took place on Saturday, February 1950 and Stockport were at home to the First Division leaders. With a 27,833 crowd (and scores of gatecrashers too, according to reports) the gate receipts were a pleasing £4,200. On a bright and dry but windy day, with the pitch in decent condition despite recent heavy rainfall, the sell-out crowd was treated to a fine match. 'It only goes to show that this cup-tie business is a great leveller,' said the *Liverpool Echo*. It was an engrossing spectacle, with underdogs County putting the First Division-topping visitors on the defensive for most of the first half and early parts of the second. Indeed, with Herd getting brought down in the Liverpool penalty area, the hosts should have been awarded a spot kick soon after the break. To add insult to injury, from close range, following something of a scramble in the Stockport goalmouth, Willie Fagan opened the scoring for Liverpool within minutes of the incident. And in the 70th minute, Albert Stubbins finished neatly to add the Reds' second and, what would prove to be, the decisive goal. Herd, with a header from a corner in the 90th minute, pulled one back for County but, sadly, they were out of the FA Cup after such a valiant run.

Les was flattered by their interest but did not want the move. He was playing regularly for Stockport's first-team whereas at Anfield there would be slim chance of even a few appearances for Liverpool's starting eleven, especially with renowned forwards there such as Stubbins, Liddell and Fagan. No, if he transferred to the Reds he would be a reserve forward at best, a mere bit-part player, the upheaval of a move to Merseyside was not worth the risk.

League-wise, Stockport County finished tenth in their division in 1949/50. All in all it was Les's best season so far, appearing 37 times in the league and scoring 13 goals, with three FA Cup goals in six appearances.

In June 1950, Les married Nora Pickersgill. They received the wedding present of an inscribed clock from the Stockport County players and staff. Their home was a council house, 9 Woodbank Avenue, in the Bredbury district of Stockport. They didn't own a car, primarily because Les always walked to work as it was less than three miles away. Treks of three miles were nothing for a fitness fanatic like Les, even a few times per day. The Cockers loved speedway racing – watching rather than participating – and were regular spectators at Belle Vue in Manchester. Speedway had been rising in popularity in 1930s England, only for the sporting landscape to be disrupted by war. The 1950s speedway scene enjoyed a post-war rise and was one of the most-watched spectator sports around. This was a time when, perhaps, there were fewer leisure options in general British life but people found more to do. Any alcohol-drinking culture, for instance, was minor in comparison to cinema, dance halls and 'plain old' cafes.

Back to football. The 1950/51 season was a slight comedown for Stockport, finishing tenth with 48 points. Les played 44 league games and scored 11 goals, appearing twice in the FA Cup and scoring just the once. In March 1951 the main contributor to this book, Dave Cocker, was born.

In the last match of that season, May 1951, Alec Herd made English football history by playing alongside his son, David Herd, just 17 at the time, in the 2–0 win against Hartlepools United. It was cited as the first time a father and son had featured together in the same league side. He would complete fewer than 20 matches for the club before being snapped up by First Division Arsenal who bought him for around £10,000. At Highbury, he really made a name for himself with the Gunners.

In the second week of November 1951, it was reported in the local press that Les had gone into hospital to have his appendix removed. Quite incredibly, the appendicitis had been diagnosed before the August start of the football season but it had not troubled him during training or when playing. The same newspaper, the *Stockport Advertiser*, then advised, on 21 December, that he was due to play for Stockport's reserves the following day, just over six weeks after his operation. No self-respecting footballer enjoys being injured and being out of the first team, but such a swift return to action is quite something. Still, when the team is doing well without you, the motivation to return and augment that success intensifies, and Les was clearly champing at the figurative bit to get back. He made it, and that 1951/52 campaign saw a fine effort from the team, finishing third with 59 points, behind champions Lincoln City and second-placed Grimsby Town. Les made 34 league appearances and scored three goals. Oddly enough, thanks to farcical league fixture scheduling common for the time, Stockport played three games against the top two in four days across the Easter bank holiday of 1952: on the Saturday at home to Lincoln, sandwiched in between the brace of league matches against Grimsby on Good Friday and Easter Monday.

The following season began well for the team and for Les personally, scoring in the first minute of the new campaign in a 4-1 win over Chester, proclaimed as the quickest-ever opening goal of a season for County. However, they would prove to be 'consistently inconsistent', with that opening win and two impressive 6-1 victories their only three out of the first 11 league games. And then serious upheaval occurred thanks to First Division Huddersfield Town luring manager Andy Beattie away. It was an opportunity he felt he could not decline, plus the pay was much higher than his Stockport wages.

Beattie's replacement at Edgeley Park, two months into the season, was Dick Duckworth, who had relinquished the same role at York City. Now, the following events might all have been entirely unrelated to Beattie's departure, but it's unlikely. In September 1952, the *Stockport Advertiser* stated that Les had submitted a written transfer request to the Stockport board of directors (which was accepted) before a 2-2 draw at Rochdale, while in October a letter purportedly from a 'Lythgoe, AP' to the same newspaper alleged player unrest at the club. Perhaps the allegation was brought on by the arrival of a new manager, but it was an unwelcome slight regardless of the reason or motive. The suggestion prompted a collective response from the players, and so the *Advertiser* published a signed letter from all 27 part-time and full-time professionals stating, 'We the undersigned players of Stockport County resent the untrue statements under the name of Lythgoe AP. To say that the

County players are not a happy family off the field of play is a wicked insinuation.'

Les remained at the club but that 1952/53 season was a disappointing one in terms of league performance, with Stockport finishing 11th on 47 points. He played in just 19 league games and scored five goals, and in the FA Cup made three appearances without scoring. Brighter fortunes for the club, however, came in the Cheshire Bowl, County triumphing again with a 3-1 win over Chester in the final.

During the run-up to the 1953/54 season, on 17 July 1953 it was reported that Les had been sold to Accrington Stanley, also of the Third Division (North), for a 'probable four-figure fee'. The end of an era and the beginning of a new one. Accrington fixed Les up with a council house, his new home in the Huncoat area of the town, around two miles – a few minutes' walk – from the Peel Park stadium, Les's new place of employment. Luck of the draw would have it that his home debut would be against Stockport, and Les scored the decisive goal for Accrington ten minutes from the end in the 2-1 win. With Stanley he was one of very few Englishmen to appear regularly in the Scots-heavy first eleven during Walter Galbraith's term as manager and in one game it is said he was the only Englishman. Classed as a 'utility forward' by this stage, he nonetheless demonstrated his versatility by appearing in most positions during his stay at Peel Park. It is said that he even took over the goalkeeper's jersey for Stanley's reserves at Lancaster in August 1955. That first season was rather inauspicious with Stanley finishing 15th, with five points fewer than Stockport and five places lower. The team, however, improved markedly for the following campaign and Les enjoyed an outstanding season, scoring 21 goals in 41 appearances. This included hat-tricks in successive matches in January 1955.

While Les was with Accrington, Nora gave birth to Stephen in 1954, and four years later to Ian in 1958; Ian was born in Clitheroe and so had the affectionate nickname of 'the Clitheroe kid'. Around 1956, Les had finally gone modern by acquiring a Panther motorbike plus two-seater sidecar to transport the Cockers when needed, including for holidays and weekends away. He still walked to work more often than not. What with his Accrington career, in addition to his FA studies, the family excursions were few and far between. Eldest son Dave remembers one particular family trip, with Les driving and Nora riding pillion, and Dave in the front seat of the sidecar with toddler Stephen behind him. Les drove them to the seaside to see Blackpool's glorious illuminations. After the return journey, the parents were furious to discover that Stephen had somehow managed to open the little back window of the sidecar and thrown his shoes out.

An important part of Les's move to Accrington Stanley was the agreement that the club would pay for his Football Association coaching courses, plus the Treatment of Injuries course to help him progress into physiotherapy. Since 1946, when Walter Winterbottom had been made the first-ever manager of the England team, the FA had endeavoured to develop football, regarding it as their duty to steer the sport into new eras, especially as England had the best team and association football was an English invention, apparently. Nothing pompous about that at all, of course. However, with a disastrous England performance at the 1950 World Cup in Brazil, and two humiliations at the hands of Hungary in 1953 and again a year later, it gradually dawned on the FA that there was much, much more work to do.

Walter Winterbottom

Tall and bespectacled, Walter Winterbottom was chosen in 1946 by Stanley Rous, the head of the FA, to be England's director of coaching. The role, ostensibly, was twinned with being the England manager too, without him actually picking the team. That was the responsibility of a selection committee, as it had been for decades. It might seem odd that Winterbottom was given the role despite having no previous football managerial experience, but no odder than selectors picking the national side without having played the game at any significant standard. At least Winterbottom had played professionally, for Manchester United in the 1930s, his debut coming against Leeds United, but medical issues and then World War Two halted his playing career.

While his management record of England does not exactly gleam with glorious achievement, he indubitably helped the national game develop, with innovations such as forming the England B team, as well as the under-23, youth and schoolboy platforms, together with creating national coaching courses via the Lilleshall Hall National Recreation Centre in Lilleshall, Shropshire. Those courses culminated in FA preliminary and full coaching badges for the students. Les was one of the earliest to benefit in that respect, together with other soccer luminaries such as Bill Nicholson, Bill Shankly, Bob Paisley, Johnny Carey, Joe Fagan, Don Howe, Jimmy Sirrel, Frank Swift, Alan Brown, Ron Greenwood, Joe Mercer, Jimmy Hill and Bobby Robson.

To aid his project, Winterbottom persuaded some of his international players to take the courses which led to exams for the FA's preliminary and full coaching badges. Les was not an England regular but he was ambitious and highly intuitive; he *knew* his future after playing football lay in coaching it. He wasn't alone; the courses led, in a way, to a 'new wave' for English football, with the places eagerly taken up. This was a time when coaches were often called 'bucket and sponge' men, as if they possessed minimal skill and were there just to tend to injured players on the pitch. Quite insulting, really. The course took three to four years, with modules held at different venues around the country, not solely at Lilleshall. Incidentally, part of the course was held at Leeds Carnegie in the Headingley area of the city. Les would forge great friendships with some of the lads on the courses, particularly Paisley, Shankly, Fagan, Busby and Carey, all strong and like-minded individuals who would have huge impact on English football.

Les completed his studies and gained his full coaching qualifications in May 1957 to become Accrington Stanley coach. He had by that time effectively retired from playing but was then re-signed as a player in September 1957 to help out in an injury crisis. By the end of his playing days for Stanley, Les had made a total of 130 league and cup appearances for the club and scored 50 goals.

The demise of Accrington Stanley

In 1960, due to financial difficulties reported to be approaching £30,000 overall – not a huge debt even for that era of time – they were relegated to the Fourth Division, which had been formed in 1958 to end regionalisation of the old Third Division. Stanley only managed to complete one full season in the Fourth Division due to the financial problems continuing. During the following season, the board sent a letter of resignation to the Football League, only to regret their actions almost straight away as the directors then came up with a plan to try and rescue the situation. But the resignation had already been accepted by the League Committee and their secretary, Alan Hardaker, on 11 March, near the close of the 1961/62 season; they would be replaced by Oxford United. So that was that, their record for the season was expunged and their ignominious exit confirmed with what, over time, has widely been regarded as the end of Accrington Stanley. Strictly speaking, that was not entirely true and, thankfully, there remained sufficient spirit and determination within the community and the Stanley supporters to keep their club going, albeit at a lower-league status. The Accrington phoenix would rise from the ashes in the future.

David Lloyd

Born in March 1947, David Lloyd is a former Lancashire and England cricketer, and umpire, possibly better known for his later career as a cricket commentator and pundit. In his playing days he was a skilled cricketer, while in his subsequent work he often showed good technique in gently taking the mickey out of Yorkshire folk, too. Somehow this Lancastrian lampoons the Yorkshire accent. How he has the nerve to mock any of the various Tyke twangs, I do not know! I can only surmise he has never listened to himself. And, dear reader, he has a fine accent and 'delivery'. A less well-known fact about David is that he played football at semi-professional level in the 1960s, for none other than his hometown club, Accrington Stanley. He retired from commentary work in December 2021, a few months after I interviewed him for this book. Born in 1947, he was a Stanley fan from very early on and remembers Les affectionately. Lloyd's affinity with the club remains strong, though they are, respectfully, relatively small (no surprise for a town with a population in the thirty thousands) and the healthy community spirit is essential in helping to keep them thriving. Lloyd's nickname is 'Bumble' but I got the impression he only really approves of that moniker when it's his friends calling him it. I know we Yorkshire folk should all be instinctively against Lancastrians, but damn it, I really enjoyed hearing those famous tones addressing me over the phone.

The first revelation for me was that he currently lives in Yorkshire. 'My wife's from York,' he told me. 'She supports York City and works for Lancashire cricket.'

David Lloyd at the Accrington Stanley v Fulham FA Cup tie – Crown Ground, January 2010.

'I'm surprised we let you in.'

'Oh, I'm adopted.'

I then asked him about his links to Accrington Stanley. 'I played for Stanley when they went out of the Football League, and got paid a bob or two. We were in the Lancashire Combination so we were playing teams like Marine, New Brighton, Skelmersdale and all that lot. When I played for Stanley I played up front somewhere, like inside-left. I was only young so course I got absolutely clattered, kicked all over the field, on a regular basis.'

Was he any good as a footballer? 'Yeah I was all right. I finished up playing for Rossendale United, for quite some time.'

From his perspective, what was the story behind Accrington Stanley going out of business? 'Well, there was no money of course, and there was no support due to real apathy in the town, the team wasn't playing well and the lack of funding meant we weren't able to get the players and the team wasn't winning matches. The best time was when Walter Galbraith was manager – 1953 to 58 – and that was a good team. For certain, Les Cocker was in that team.'

He's always had close ties to the club? 'The Stanley pitch was called Peel Park, and I went to Peel Park School. As my dad did, and all the family. Peel Park is literally next to the football ground. Stanley owned one of these houses and some of the players would lodge there. My auntie Edith cleaned there. I lived in Water Street and the players, on their way to the ground, would walk past our house, and some of them would be carrying their boots. We had some great centre-forwards, for example George Stewart, George Hudson and Les Cocker. All of them three were good headers of the ball.

'At matches, I would stand behind the top end goal, the coppice end. The Stanley plan would be that Les would kick off, he'd give it to the inside-forward, and he'd give it to one of the half-backs then. As soon as Les gave the ball to the inside-forward he'd set off at a rate of knots up the field, and then the half-back would launch the ball at the opposition goalkeeper. And Les would just clatter straight into him, that's the first thing that happened because you could, you were allowed, to charge the goalie in that era. Now you just need to look at them sternly and they get a foul! Even when the goalie had the ball in his hands you could have a go at him in those days.'

What was Les like as a player? 'I have strong recollection of Les. He was a marauding centre-forward, I mean fearless, all action, all effort, he put himself about, he'd get stuck in. Like Trevor Ford down in Wales. Yeah, he was a dirty bugger but a really nice bloke. Les was notorious, he liked to "engage"!'

What about his own football career? 'I was a schoolboy footballer and Stanley had their eye on me so I'd go train with them. Les was involved as a coach then, too. He was just nice, a really nice fella and an encouraging fella at the same time. He'd spend time helping us improve. To be honest, they were all just a good bunch of blokes at Stanley. Like Willie McInnes in goal. Bert Scott and Terry Tye. Joe Devlin too, a winger. And after Willie McInnes's time, Tommy McQueen was the goalkeeper, he was Gordon McQueen's dad. We had a youth team. The year would be, 1963, 64? Not sure; it was after Stanley got thrown out of the Football League, and we, the youth team, were drawn away to Leeds, and they beat us 1-0 I think, and I hit the post. Even though we lost, it was a fabulous result for us. Les had moved to Leeds by then of course, and he and Don Revie were on the touchline, watching, and Leeds were a top, top team, obviously on the up as a club. It was a big deal for us and we were proud to have put up such a good fight.

'As well as becoming a very respected coach, Les was really affectionate, a lovely bloke, dedicated to the sport. And, when he was a player, a dirty bugger! I thought he was great, I'd go to watch them every week. He gives you, I mean *us* here, a real sense of pride, the pride of Stanley, going on to represent England as well as he did.'

* * *

During his playing career at Stanley, Les played in various positions in attack, as an inside-forward or outside-left or outside-right. That first season with the club was just about acceptable, the team finishing 15th but, after that, they seemed to 'click' wonderfully well, not only entertaining the fans but also challenging for divisional honours. In the subsequent four seasons, Accrington came second, third, third and second, and then, in 1958, the Football League formed a new Fourth Division, together with the new Third Division. The 12 top-placed teams of each of the two regional third tiers went into the Third Division, while the bottom 12 of each thus formed the Fourth. Perhaps it was a rude awakening for Stanley as, in the new Third Division's first term, 1958/59, they finished 19th out of the 24 teams.

Meanwhile, further south in England, but further north in terms of Football League tables, Luton Town were having an exciting time in the First Division. They were in the lower half of the table but had reached their first FA Cup Final, led by Syd Owen, the 36-year-old former England centre-half. His form had been so impressive all season that he had been named Footballer of the Year by the Football Writers' Association, a splendid accolade. Luton's manager had been Dally Duncan but he left the club in October 1958 before the excellent FA Cup run had even started. Owen, together with Luton's directors, in an arrangement quite similar to England's selection committee, had, effectively, managed the team ever since.

Sadly for Luton, who shared the same nickname of the Hatters with Stockport, they did not play particularly well in the final and were comfortably beaten by Nottingham Forest. Forest, for two-thirds of the match, had been reduced to ten men due to a serious injury to Roy Dwight (a cousin of Elton John whose birth name was Reg Dwight) in the first half. By then, though, they had scored two early goals and while Luton gradually went on to dominate, they managed to score just the one goal, midway through the second half. Following the final, Owen was officially made Luton manager but he had already informed the board of directors that he wanted a professional trainer-coach to assist him. The position was advertised and Les was one of numerous applicants, but one immediate snag was that, despite Les being a well-known 'lower-league' player, Owen professed to never having heard of him. After reading Les's application letter though, he decided he need look no further as he was perfect for the job.

'The first thing that impressed me, and I can still visualise it now, was the firmness of his handwriting,' Owen said a few years later. 'I sensed that here was a fellow who knew his own mind, who believed in himself, who put his heart into the words he wrote. That handwriting was like the man himself – unshakeable. It simply oozed character. And the letter itself made no bones about the writer's faith in his own ability. The words said, boldly and clearly, exactly how he would do the job of a trainer. They listed his qualifications, crisp and concise. In effect, they said that Leslie Cocker knew he would be a success in the job. All he required was the chance to prove it to Luton.'

In the same publication, the *Leeds United Official Handbook 1963/64*, Les commented, 'I had determined to prepare myself for the day I had to quit playing, and that day comes to every footballer, if he faces up to the realities of life. Age catches up with everyone. When Syd asked me to join him on the staff at Luton, I snapped up the chance, and I've blessed that day many times since, for when we teamed up together, it was the start of a partnership which has lasted for years. Those who still remain sceptical about coaching are missing out.'

Officially, he started his new role as Luton's assistant trainer on 10 August 1959, but had actually been offered the job before the FA Cup Final. He had no involvement with the FA Cup adventure and wasn't even invited to the match at Wembley.

The new Cocker family home was on Shaftesbury Avenue in Luton. Dave remembers their time at Luton with not a lot of fondness due to the locals' apparent dislike of outsiders!

Syd Owen

Syd was born in Aston, Birmingham, in 1922. Birmingham City had beaten Preston North End in signing him as an amateur in October 1945. He made just five Second Division appearances as a left-half for the team before Luton bought him for £1,500 in June 1947 and developed him into a fine centre-half. During his 12-year Hatters career, he represented England on three occasions. It is not unkind to describe him as something of a 'bruff Brummie', as he wasn't one to suffer fools gladly and would always demand 100 per cent effort from his players. This attitude could be, and was, regarded by some as overzealous or simply too hard, but Owen always saw his role as getting the best out of players, regardless of their feelings about the matter.

When he was made Luton's manager, it was evident that he had taken charge of an ageing side and one that had suffered a demoralising defeat in the club's greatest occasion. And they had lost his exemplary services as a player, too. As a result, Luton had a disastrous 1959/60 season with Owen in charge, finishing bottom and being relegated to the Second Division after five years at the top level. He resigned on 23 April 1960 but took up a coaching role at Leeds United in the next month. Funnily enough, Leeds had been relegated with Luton, having finished second from bottom. It would not be long before Owen recommended Les Cocker to Leeds manager Jack Taylor.

3

Leeds and England dreaming

JACK TAYLOR had been in charge of the side when Leeds were relegated with Luton to the Second Division in April 1960. It had been a miserable season but Taylor was determined to redeem himself and rebuild the club as best he could. Ultimately, it did not work but in the ensuing months he would bring in important personnel to the club such as coach Syd Owen, Bob English and Cyril Partridge, as well as Les Cocker around July 1960.

With the move to West Yorkshire complete, the new Cocker family home was to be in Kirkdale Gardens in Lower Wortley, a short walk from Leeds' Elland Road stadium, enabling Les to walk to and from work as often as he liked. The Cockers were next door to Leeds player Noel Peyton, while Grenville Hair and Jimmy Ashall had only recently moved out.

Les's journey on foot each day was probably the simplest part of his early time at the club, for it was not a happy place of employment for many, and things were not going well on or off the pitch. There was a distinct lack of professionalism among certain older players, with some appearing to not care too much about the team, and Taylor considered as being too weak a manager. Owen and Les had their work cut out if they were going to improve matters.

Eric Smith was a player who prided himself in his professionalism and never-say-die attitude, the calibre of man who was at his best when the going got tough and who Les hoped he could rely on to help improve the club. Smith signed from Celtic in May 1960 but broke his leg in just his second Leeds game, the following August. He recovered well and returned to first-team action on New Year's Eve in 1960. He would be a big influence at the club at a time when versatility, experience and determination were in dire need. Les grew to respect him immensely.

On their early days at Elland Road, Owen commented, 'It was frustrating because there was only a limited amount of work we could do with the senior players. They were set in their ways. It was different with the youngsters, although manager Jack Taylor sometimes felt that we were inclined to push them too hard. I couldn't see that, I just felt that a lot of really hard work at the start of their career was bound to stand them in good stead in the long run.'

The view that Owen, and thus, by association, Les pushed young players too hard in training would be heard occasionally over the years. I would suggest that the two men genuinely always wanted the best for the youngsters in their charge, but

Owen's approach and demeanour undoubtedly could – and did – cause upset. He was not the warmest or most outwardly encouraging of men, and quick, probably too quick for most people, to criticise. Les, on the other hand, had his own, more personable and infinitely more respected methods, to help lads fulfil their potential and realise their dreams. The business of football was undoubtedly tough and a player's journey commonly littered with harsh words and bruising lessons, but it was felt that Owen was perhaps too eager at times to provide them.

The club brought in a new team doctor to Elland Road, too – 30-year-old Dr Ian Adams. 'Doc Adams' had joined his father's practice in Beeston, Leeds, in 1959, after two years of national service where he had passed the Airborne Selection course to become a captain in 2 Para, serving in Cyprus and Jordan. Tall and slim, and usually wearing a suit, he cut a distinguished figure, not unlike (in my opinion) the famous record producer George Martin. Along with lots of other people in Beeston, Dr Adams was my family doctor for several years in the late 1960s and early 70s.

Born in October 1943, 17-year-old County Durham lad Norman Hunter joined the Leeds ground staff in November 1960, hoping to make the grade as a professional footballer. In later years, in his autobiography, he wrote, 'Les Cocker wasn't all that big but he was as tough as they come. On the face of it, he and Syd Owen were the ideal pair to put the discipline back into Leeds United but boy did they have some problems. Syd had more fights and arguments than Les because his attitude was, "You do it my way or not at all."'

By April 1961, having signed a professional contract, Norman purchased one of the club houses. It was in Kirkdale Gardens, just a couple of doors away from the Cocker household. Norman's mother moved to Leeds to look after him and also be the landlady for other players who lodged there, Terry Yorath and Tommy Henderson. According to Dave Cocker, Henderson had a record player fitted in his Triumph Herald, screwed in underneath the car's dashboard. Tommy had little knowledge about pop music though and so asked to borrow some of Dave's vinyl singles to play in the car. Dave obliged but took them back a while later as Tommy had simply thrown them on the car's floor after playing them. Dave also remembers Hunter buying himself a car, a salmon pink Vauxhall Viva with registration number ALE999B.

One famous – 'infamous' was possibly more appropriate at that time – player present at the club before Les arrived was Jack Charlton. The opinionated, unruly, one-man awkward squad from Ashington, Northumberland seemed to be on a football path of self-destruction. Only he talked sense and only he knew what was best for him. He was no less troublesome by 1960 when Les started working for the club. In his own words, Charlton admitted that when it came to Les, he was just 'facetious and nasty'. Soon after arriving, Les found himself being goaded by Charlton, with sneers along the lines of, 'What are we doing then, Cocker?'; 'You know best, Cocker';

and so on. Eventually Les had heard enough of the sarcasm and stopped Charlton in the car park to have a stern chat with him, 'Listen, if you don't stop calling me Cocker ...' 'Well, tell me what you'd bloody well like to be called if it's not by your name,' interrupted the player. Les replied, 'I've got a bloody handle, you know, and it's Les.'

Gerry Francis

Another player already at Elland Road when Les joined was Gerry Francis. In football terms, Gerry would not achieve the same success as Jack Charlton would, but he is now regarded as a real pioneer in the sport nonetheless. He was Leeds' first black player, with great skills, flair, athleticism and work ethic. In addition, he possessed a pleasant, positive demeanour and was a good person and character to have around the place. Back in Johannesburg, he had always preferred playing on hard, virtually grassless surfaces where players' boots had bars rather than studs on the soles. Born in 1933 to an African mother and an Indian father in Johannesburg, South Africa, he was

signed by Leeds manager Raich Carter in 1957 after a family friend sponsored him to pay for his flight over for a trial. Gerry made his first-team debut against Birmingham City at Elland Road at the end of November that year.

'Les was a very good coach and trainer,' Gerry advised in recent interview. 'He was also very strict. If you did not train as hard as he thought you could, Les would be tough on you. He would train you one-on-one and by the time he was finished with you, you could hardly walk! He would say, "Lads, pull your socks up or the next time will be worse." And that is why, after Les had joined the club, all the players started to train hard, so that they would not have to do a one-on-one with Les. I benefited a lot from Les's training as it made me a better player. I visited Les and Syd's homes for tea every now and then and we would chat about football, especially the style of football played in South Africa. And Don Revie used to pick my brains, asking about how we played the game in South Africa. They were all really interested to hear of the differences between England and my own country. I wasn't a winger in Africa, I was an inside-forward, I was a man who used to fetch and carry, fetch and carry, that's what an inside-forward did. Raich Carter put me on the wing so that, when I got the ball, I could draw defenders out away from goal. Then, as I could beat so many men, I just had to put the ball in and let the guys in the middle score the goals. And that is what happened.'

As Leeds manager for the 1958/59 season, Bill Lambton made too few good decisions in his time. There was scant respect from the players for him too, and if a manager does not have the respect of his playing staff then it is, almost certainly, a lost cause. One of his good decisions is rather trivial, really: he was the man responsible for the 'KEEP FIGHTING' sign hanging on the Leeds dressing-room wall while two other decisions proved to be life-changing for Leeds. Lambton signed 31-year-old Don Revie and a young Scotsman called Billy Bremner. Revie arrived from Sunderland in November 1958 for £12,000. Although a former England international and Footballer of the Year, realistically he was past his best and in the twilight of his career. Therefore, in terms of on-the-pitch affairs, the move was not a particular success and Lambton remained deeply unpopular as manager. He was succeeded by Jack Taylor but he failed to stop the rot and things went from bad to worse.

By March 1961, approaching his 34th birthday, Revie knew his playing days would be over sooner rather than later and was looking to get into management. He had applied for the player-manager role at Bournemouth. He had even asked Leeds director and soon-to-be new chairman Harry Reynolds to write him a reference, and had told Leeds teammate Peter McConnell that if he got the job then he wanted to take McConnell with him and make him Bournemouth's captain. On 13 March, however, with Leeds flirting with the lower reaches of Division Two and air of discontent continuing to darken Elland Road, director Harry Reynolds asked Taylor to resign. Taylor did so, prompting incumbent chairman Sam

Bolton to declare Leeds as managerless again. Four days after Taylor's exit, Reynolds insisted Revie be given the job of player-manager as there was no one better to fill the role.

Don Revie

In addition to his reputation as an intelligent 'deep-lying centre-forward', Revie was well known for his resilience too. Having overcome a career-threatening ankle injury during the 1946/47 season for Leicester, in 1949 and just one week before he had been due to play in the FA Cup Final against Wolves, he broke his nose and suffered a nasal haemorrhage caused by a burst vein. The loss of blood was so severe that it was not just his career under threat but his very life, needing an urgent blood transfusion to finally remedy the issue. A clear sign of his astuteness was demonstrated while at Maine Road with Manchester City, from 1951 to 1956, with a new tactic called, flatteringly, 'the Revie Plan'. Revie sought neither recognition nor praise for the plan, primarily because he was not solely responsible for it at the club; other personnel were involved, and the plan had stemmed from the feted Hungary team who had thrashed England in 1953 and 1954.

As his reign as manager began, one of the first issues for Revie to address was whether or not to take on the young South African, Albert Johanneson. Revie's predecessor, Taylor, had been in charge when the arrangements had been made for Johanneson to travel to Leeds all the way from Johannesburg, to try out for the playing squad. Two of the first Leeds people

Albert would meet were Les Cocker and Syd Owen. One of Les's first jobs with Albert was to find him a pair of studded football boots as he had never played in any before; it had always been barefoot or some kind of plimsolls before. Dave Cocker, meanwhile, went in goal at Fullerton Park while Albert took shots and set-piece kicks at him. Worryingly, within days of his arrival from South Africa, Les had to break the news to him that Taylor had resigned as manager and that his successor was not yet known. Les, however, assured him that he and Owen would recommend to the new manager, whoever it was to be, that Leeds sign Albert on.

Leeds did take him on, and Johanneson would become the second black player in the club's history to represent the first team. Revie commented on the signing some time later, 'I had my doubts about him and, to be truthful, it was Les Cocker who finally persuaded me that Albert was of sufficient quality to represent the club. Les said that Albert would light up every football pitch in Europe with his blistering pace and ball control. In signing him I was helping my own reputation as a manager with real vision, and a new, international image for the football club.'

Somehow, in spite of the team's woes and the disorganised state of affairs at Elland Road, since the sale of the great John Charles to Juventus in 1957, the club had occasionally recruited very well in certain areas. By March 1961, it could even be said that Revie had been blessed from the outset of his managerial career to have such a team of backroom staff already at his disposal, men with experience and wisdom who knew how crucial their teamwork could and should be for their joint cause: Owen, English, Partridge and, of course, Cocker. In addition, the Leeds scouting network had proven its worth over the recent years too, and it would increase the 'production line' marvellously well. What's more, Revie was able to bring back the popular Maurice Lindley to the club, as chief scout this time. All of these men had the shared goal of building Leeds, under Revie and chairman Harry Reynolds, into a true and dynamic football force. Even with arguably the greatest player on Earth, John Charles, in the side during the 1950s, the club had barely even skirted heights of glory. Revie would prove himself to be an excellent manager but it is unlikely he would have achieved so much without these men of such dedication and devotion at his side.

Leeds had famously benefited from the scouting work of Jack Pickard in Swansea, crucial in bringing Charles to the club. Those were the days when Leeds' talent spotters would trawl the land in hope of discovering potential greats and then invite their choices to try out at Elland Road. Boys would arrive in the summer, usually carrying belongings and football boots in suitcases or wrapped in paper, always carrying their football dreams in their heads and hearts. Their travel would have been paid for by the club's scout, and the board and lodgings for a week, sometimes two, more often than not in the local area of Beeston, taken care of by the club too.

Jack Charlton, speaking about the beginning of the Revie era, said, 'Part of this new regime was a much greater emphasis on fitness, something that had long been ignored in professional football where training usually meant nothing more than a few laps of the ground.' There is absolutely no doubt that Revie's fully qualified trainer-coach, Les, contributed hugely to the new training methods at Elland Road. Not only was there a greater emphasis on fitness but the coaches made sure that training sessions were more interesting, more competitive and more fun.

Norman Hunter was one of the United youngsters who, it was felt by Revie and the backroom team, needed to 'beef up', both in physique and in playing style. In his book, Hunter recounted this tale, 'We used to train on Fullerton Park, a piece of land adjacent to the Elland Road stadium with a corrugated iron fence around two sides of the playing area. Later, the club seeded it but initially the surface was shale. Les would play in the practice matches and he used to clatter into you, sending you sprawling. Often, you would end up hitting the fencing. I think it was his way of trying to toughen us up. On one occasion, shortly after I had made it into the first team, the ball dropped between Les and me soon after kick-off. I thought, right mate, this is payback time. I charged in and hit him with everything I had. I put him into the air and into the fencing. I wondered what I had let myself in for but Les looked up at me with a huge smile, as if to say, "Great, you've learnt, you've got the idea now." Then he turned to John Hawksby and gave him the biggest rollicking of his young life for not having passed the ball to him more accurately!'

Willie Bell, signed as a left-half in 1960 but who would become a fine left-back for the side, recalled early changes at the club once Revie was in charge, 'I remember when Don took over. We went for pre-season training and I thought we were just going to kick a ball around, but no, instead we were divided into teams of six, and points were awarded for running, for relay races, even for carrying huge telegraph poles the length of the field. You do that twice and you can't move the next day! I think at Leeds we trained harder than any other side.'

In the 1920s, there had been a Leeds United player named Jimmy Frew. At 28 years old, the Scottish full-back had transferred from Heart of Midlothian for £200 in June 1920. He would go on to make 99 league and cup appearances for Leeds before joining Bradford City in 1924. What has this got to do with Les, you might ask. The answer is, 'not a lot really' but, more seriously, Les's myriad of duties at one stage included the acquisition of all the kits to be worn each season by the first team, reserves and juniors, not forgetting the goalkeepers' shirts, and all the training gear for every player and coaching staff also. Frew, since retiring from the game in 1926 due to injury, eventually moved into the sports outfitting business. He would become the official supplier to Leeds and his James H. Frew Limited premises, where customers could buy 'the best sports and skating equipment', were situated on Harehills Corner in

Leeds 8. Les would be a regular visitor and Jimmy, without doubt, would have greatly looked forward to seeing him.

Les would advise him what was needed – always an all-white strip times three, and usually an all-blue one. There was possibly a differently coloured third kit required too, and it seems that in the second half of the decade, *red* was arranged (yes I know, what were they thinking?!) With his orders book full, Frew would order all the kits in, including the occasional short-sleeved shirt versions if any of the players had specific preferences. The work hadn't quite finished – each shirt then had to have a number on the back, and they, apparently, were ordered from sportswear manufacturers Umbro, probably the largest football kit suppliers around at the time, and then there was the club crest needed for each shirt as well. These badges, consisting of a Leeds owl on a perch, were specially made as cloth patches in Leeds, it is believed, and then the lovely ladies in the Elland Road laundry were tasked with sewing them on to all the shirts. Everything was bought by the club, and that included the footballs, boots, training equipment and so on, this was a considerable length of time before sponsorship and commercialisation would pervade the sport.

1960/61

Leeds were toiling in the Second Division when Revie took over in mid-March 1961, and there was a distinct possibility they would be in a fight against relegation to the Third Division unless they got their act together. Revie had nine league games to turn the ship around, so to speak. His reign did not start well, a defeat away to Portsmouth followed by a home defeat to Sheffield United (though the Blades would go on to win promotion). With two points for a win and one point for a draw, avoiding defeat was the crucial factor. A renewed emphasis on defence was not a pretty sight for the hardy few loyal followers but it was necessary, and while his first win only came at the seventh attempt, a 7-0 thrashing of lowly Lincoln, draws against Luton, Swansea, Stoke and Scunthorpe (in the penultimate game) were all good results. At the season's end, Revie's Leeds had finished 14th out of 22 teams but only five points clear of the highest relegated team, Portsmouth, who went down with Lincoln. It had been too close for comfort and things could only get better next season.

For Les, life became even busier from November 1961 as he became trainer to the England under-23 side, with Walter Winterbottom still the manager. Professional football players needed to be ultra-dedicated to their profession, but they were all given time off each week during the season. Managers, trainers, coaches, even physios, however, rarely had a moment's rest. It was a sign of Les's standing in the game that Winterbottom's England took him on, those coaching qualifications had proved their worth. It is easy to evaluate this as evidence of all of his hard work paying dividends – the harder you work at something, the likelier you are to succeed – and success in football often signifies an increase in work and commitment to one's employers. Could the increase in workload for individual backroom staff be detrimental to their home lives? Once Revie had taken over at Leeds and instilled new ideas and stronger work ethic, on and off the pitch, certain men like Les will have had little time to spend at home each week.

Les's new England role officially started with a victory against Israel at Elland Road on Thursday, 9 November, though the under-23s (also known as 'Young England' in the media) drew in a friendly against Huddersfield Town on the Tuesday. At this stage, there were no Leeds players involved with England, at any level. The team against Israel included Gordon West in goal, Brian Labone and Bobby Moore in defence, and Johnny Byrne, who scored twice in the 7-1 win, at centre-forward. Israel actually scored first but their lead didn't last long. A crowd of 12,419 attended, similar to Leeds' average home attendances for the season. England's under-23 coach was none other than former centre-half and 105-cap England record holder Billy Wright. Wright was wanted by Arsenal to be their new coach but he turned it down, according to the media, as he had expectations of replacing Winterbottom, who was expected to end his reign – after the 1962 World Cup in Chile – to replace Sir Stanley Rous as secretary of the Football Association. Notwithstanding, Wright was still in charge of the under-23s by the time they beat their Netherlands counterparts 5-2 in Rotterdam on 29 November. For Les, the journeys to and from the Netherlands were betwixt Leeds matches against Walsall and away at Derby County.

1961/62

Leeds avoided relegation by a narrow margin, finishing 19th out of 22 with 36 points, just three more than the higher of the two relegated teams, Bristol Rovers. After winning their opening two league games they would win just ten more all season, four of them in the final seven weeks. Even with the promise of the young manager Revie in charge, the unthinkable had become worryingly plausible that Leeds would be relegated to the Third Division for the first time in their history. Thankfully, even with the club reportedly in debt to around £150,000, chairman Harry Reynolds continued to back his manager. And that backing was never more evident than when five foot four inches of fire and fury, Bobby Collins, was bought from First Division Everton for £25,000 (no small amount for a 31 year old) in March 1962.

With just 11 games of the season remaining, and the trap door to the Third Division beckoning, Collins made his debut at home to Swansea. He marshalled the team to victory, like a true inspirational leader, even scoring the second goal in the 2-0 win. And even though Leeds were beaten at Southampton in the next match, thanks largely to Collins's influence they remained unbeaten in their final nine, winning three and drawing six.

Although Collins actually worried people with the ferocity of his will to win, he was a model professional and became integral in the ascent of Leeds, on and off the pitch. Just as Les knew and tried to practise, everything had to be done 'right' to help the club thrive, but few men have such influence as Collins possessed to be able to bring about such transformation. Revie, Les and most of the players from that era always agreed that without Collins none of the ensuing success would even have happened.

There had been other significant new purchases too: Tommy Younger in goal, Ian Lawson up front and Cliff Mason in defence. Younger would, in Revie's words, 'play his heart out for the club' and turn in some fantastic displays, while helping Les and Owen coach the club's junior goalkeepers.

On the England under-23s' side of life, Les was on duty again straight after Leeds' home game against Plymouth on 24 February 1962. Four days later, up in Aberdeen and with Wright in charge, England beat Scotland 4-2 at Pittodrie. It was Jimmy Greaves's first representative match since returning from Italy so there was plenty of attention on the match, more than for 'normal' under-23 ties. The England party were in Aberdeen on the Tuesday, with no complaints from the travellers about the cold weather as it was actually warmer than in England. They trained at Linksfield Stadium in Aberdeen and had a practice match in which Wright and Les participated. There was never any stopping Les playing, be it training with Leeds or England, he still had 'it' and enjoyed maintaining his high physical fitness. Leeds' next fixture was away at Huddersfield on the Saturday, so the travelling continued.

The next match for the under-23s was against Turkey on Thursday, 22 March, played at Southampton's The Dell. England won 4-1. Coincidentally, Leeds had played there just five days prior.

1962/63

Only the Leeds board really wanted 'The Gentle Giant' John Charles back at Elland Road. Revie and Les would have preferred the club not to spend a record £53,000 for him. Even Charles himself was not keen; he wasn't in particularly good physical or mental condition and the drop from the top Italian league into the English Second Division was too much. Despite the encouraging end to the previous season, Leeds' start to the 1962/63 campaign was far from satisfactory and star striker Charles managed just three goals in 11 games. The move was a failure, a gamble which could have seriously damaged Revie's plans. Fortunately for Leeds, Charles was still a prized player back in Italy. Roma stumped up around £70,000 for his signature, providing Reynolds with a 'Get Out Of Jail Free card' at the same time. Another setback, struck, however, when Eric Smith broke his leg again – a double fracture – during the home league game against Chelsea in September 1962. This was a big moment for the club; Smith was an important player, as tough as they came, and a dedicated pro. Les was gutted about the situation as Smith had been a great ally and had performed heroically the previous season in the battle against relegation to the Third Division.

In terms of form, the season was something of a stop–start effort, and then the winter of the 1962/63 season struck – the infamous Big Freeze, one of the coldest periods in British history. Numerous matches had to be postponed and most teams went weeks without a league fixture, but the biggest obstacles to Leeds' promotion challenge proved to be their poor start to the campaign and their substandard away form. Just four wins on the road saw Leeds finish fifth in the Second Division with 48 points, just four behind second-placed promoted Chelsea and five behind champions Stoke City. It had been a fine season, so close but so far, and hopes were understandably high for the next one, even higher by the second league match of 1963/64.

For Les, between Leeds games against Norwich and Grimsby came another England under-23 match on Wednesday, 7 November 1962. At Plymouth Argyle's Home Park, England beat Belgium 6-1. Alf Ramsey would attend, to monitor not just the progress of certain players but also the England staff.

The under-23s' next fixture was the comfortable win against Greece on 28 November, played at Birmingham's St Andrew's ground, followed by a 0-0 stalemate with Yugoslavia at Old Trafford, Manchester. A mini-tour was arranged for the close season, meaning thousands of miles more travelling for Les, with games in Yugoslavia and Romania. Joe Mercer was now in charge of the under-23s, and the two matches saw the return to the group of Fulham's 23-year-old right-back George Cohen. England beat the Yugoslavs 4-2 in Belgrade on 29 May but lost in Bucharest, 1-0 to Romania. Little respite for Les afterwards, with Leeds undertaking a week's tour of Italy including matches against Roma – as part of the Charles deal – Cremonese Select and Prato, from 5 to 13 June.

Alf Ramsey

With England losing to Brazil in the quarter-final of the 1962 World Cup in Chile, Walter Winterbottom came in for heavy criticism from the English press. No real surprise there, though unquestionably the players and Football Association were also culpable. The England entourage did not even include a doctor, and one player, Peter Swan, could have paid heavily when he fell seriously ill with dysentery and received the wrong medical treatment in Viña del Mar. There was always a whiff of penny-pinching by the FA when it came to England matches, especially overseas. The FA 'suits' would enjoy the best accommodation and expenses, while the players had to make do with inferior hotels and allowances.

Change was needed, England had been underperforming for years. Winterbottom would resign his post and Ramsey would be confirmed as the new manager in October that year, though he formally took charge in May 1963. One of his first actions was to demand complete control over squad selections, and he got it. This led to him being referred to as England's first 'proper' manager which is a little harsh on Winterbottom as he had recommended the very same thing. Unsurprisingly, the FA hierarchy originally opposed the idea but it was crucial to Ramsey taking the job. Another surprise from Ramsey came with his assertion that England would win the next World Cup, in 1966.

John Giles

The 22-year-old joined Leeds from Matt Busby's Manchester United in August 1963, for the not inconsiderable fee of £33,000. Already established in the Republic of Ireland team from the age of 19, even at that price he would prove to be a bargain. Over the following 12 years he would play 527 times for Leeds and score 114 goals. He has contributed greatly to this book too, and he still has all that wisdom and wit, expressed as always in that marvellous Irish burr.

So, what were his reasons for leaving Manchester United to join Second Division Leeds? 'This was a very well-run club thanks to Don. Getting the right players in – if you don't sign the right players then you're not going to have a very good team. As I've said before, the signing of Bobby Collins was huge. His leadership, experience, how to train as a professional, how to look after yourself were excellent, and then they brought in the young lads – Norman, Paul Reaney, Terry Cooper – terrific, great players and they were shown how to do it, mostly by Bobby Collins as an example. You couldn't get a better example than Bobby Collins. Without Bobby I don't think it would have happened for Leeds United, the Don Revie era wouldn't have happened.'

I asked John if he would have actually signed for Leeds if Collins hadn't already been at the club, 'He was a huge influence. I knew he was there and Leeds suddenly looked like a team that was coming on, this was a team on the up and up and that was thanks to Bobby. But when you leave a club it's always a gamble, you never know what's going to happen. I was very lucky that I joined at the right time. Bobby was the man and a huge influence for everyone at the club.'

1963/64

During the 1963 tour to Italy, Billy Bremner, formerly a forward, was converted to right-half and the change just clicked for player and team. In Collins, Leeds had the obvious choice for captain but it was Jack Charlton who ran the show at the back. Even in the late 1950s, when the team was on the slide and Charlton had a reputation as something of a reckless player and 'one-man awkward squad', he was a player who Walter Winterbottom knew of as a 'possible'. And once he had recognised the fact that great professionals like Les and Owen deserved his respect and not his disdain, he understood they were the calibre of men who could help his trajectory as a player and further beyond. Charlton enrolled for FA coaching badges. And so, while Collins was the skipper, Charlton, with his tactical awareness, knowledge of the game, and his self-confidence, no doubt boosted by the FA courses, led the defence.

With striker Jim Storrie ruled out with injury, Revie brought in Alan Peacock, a superb target man, from Middlesbrough in February 1964. It was a clever purchase, but not cheap at £53,000, as Peacock went on to score eight goals in 14 games. Leeds went through the whole season unbeaten at Elland Road and lost only three league games away. Revie often showed his mettle by adjusting tactics during matches, usually away ones, and if Leeds took the lead the players understood the instruction: defend it at practically all costs. They went up as worthy champions, 63 points won out of a maximum 84, a fine achievement. They had even performed valiantly in the FA Cup, quite a rarity, losing 2-0 to defending league champions Everton in the fourth-round replay at Goodison Park in January. The teams had drawn 1-1 in a feisty Elland Road encounter.

Revie once said, 'A manager is only as good as his team. That means the backroom team as well as the 11 players who go out on the park … I also have been helped terrifically by the backroom team who work unceasingly for Leeds – Syd Owen, Les Cocker, Maurice Lindley, Bob English and Cyril Partridge and co. – what we have achieved couldn't have been done without their aid, and their loyalty … They started a job and they wanted to finish it.' His comments were not mere modesty; Leeds were truly a united organisation, on and off the field of play, and the emphases on hard work and teamwork were a life force running through the club. Every employee knew their responsibilities, and everyone had the same goal and similar ambitions, to get Leeds to the top. Revie instilled the need for unbreakable camaraderie and a spirit of close family, real ingredients for success which would be permanent features of his Leeds legacy.

On joining the club, John Giles immediately saw qualities at Elland Road which Revie worked so hard to create and which perhaps had been lacking at Old Trafford, 'When I first started at Leeds, I was on the right wing – on the right side anyway – and the way Leeds played was new to me in relation to Manchester United, and I didn't start off very well. I didn't play all that well when I started. Les was very understanding and had a few chats with me, helped me settle down in to the club. He was a big help in that way.'

Also, in his autobiography, Giles was typically keen to apportion credit for Leeds' storming promotion, 'Probably the key man was a wonderfully talented kid from South Africa called Albert Johanneson, who scored 15 goals in the Second Division campaign, a post-war record for a winger. He had amazing close control and was exceptionally quick, he was also one of the most naturally fit players I have ever seen. During the cross-country runs in pre-season training, most of us would be gasping for breath ... We would look ahead to see Albert

200 yards in front, running effortlessly and leaping to pull a leaf off an overhanging tree!'

Giles praised Owen and Les too. Owen, he said, spoke only of football but not about his own contribution to it. 'He was a football fanatic in the pure sense, a man totally devoted to the game and a hard taskmaster with the young players. But he was hard on himself too. He saw no way to achieve things other than by utter dedication and work, work, work.' He added that Les was more involved with the first team but was equally fanatical about football, 'Les would take training and work with the injured players. He was very conscientious, painstaking, all these virtues that were the bedrock of what was to come.'

I asked Giles if Les was a tough trainer to work with, perhaps even too tough? 'I would say good,' he replied. 'All the good trainers are tough but without overdoing it. Les was good, very good. As a player you need good discipline and timekeeping, for a club to be run properly. Les and Don would insist on that, there would be no messing about when it came to the running of the club. The players would have fun and mess about after training, but training was training, it was the job.

'Les took the training and everybody had to be there on time, no messing about. In all my time at Elland Road, there were very, very few times someone was late, because once you get established in the club, your timekeeping is essential. You know, discipline is important, because you've got a group of say

16 players so if one of them is late then it messes it all up for the training. It was always very disciplined, you just couldn't be late. As a group of players, for training and for matchdays, you had to be in at the set time, every time. You couldn't have one person holding everything up, and that level of discipline stemmed from Les's training. He was out there every day with us, and Les took care of the medical side of things for the players too, in the afternoons. Les was a huge contributor to the success of the club.'

Regarding that 'medical' side of Leeds, Les was interviewed in the 1960s and said, 'When I said you are always learning, if you are prepared to take the time and the trouble, I meant it. For even a full FA coaching badge isn't the be-all and end-all of things. For instance, I've taken a three-year FA course on the treatment of injuries, another aspect of the game, and in the afternoons at Elland Road I spend time helping Bob English in the treatment room. With our experience and qualifications, Syd Owen and I can interchange duties, but my main responsibility is to ensure that the players of Leeds United are fit. And I don't think anyone will argue that they're not!

'Physical fitness is regarded, rightly so, as being of extreme importance, and my job is to make sure that the first-teamers are 100 per cent up to the demands of 90 punishing minutes on a matchday. Syd is responsible for the tactical approach to a game, and between us we try to adapt the tactics to the talent at our disposal at Elland Road. So we try to pick the best out of everything we see, at world-class level, never mind club level, and utilise it all for the benefit of Leeds United. It's paid off handsomely, as our results over the past seasons show.

'And there is one more basic for success – loyalty. Maurice Lindley was 17 years with Everton, Syd was at Luton almost the whole of his playing career; I was with Stockport and Accrington. We all learnt the lesson that a player must be loyal to his club and we have applied that lesson at Leeds. I think we have succeeded, pretty well, too.'

Talking of injuries and the like, 16-year-old goalkeeper David Harvey said after injuring an arm and pulling ligaments in both knees when playing in the reserves' 6-0 defeat to Wolverhampton Wanderers, 'I was on the table the next day having treatment when along came Les Cocker who observed, "Don't worry about it too much, there'll be plenty more like that before you finish" – he was talking about the thrashing, not my aches and pains!'

Because Les lived just a couple of miles away from Elland Road, he was always happy to walk to and from work. His good friend Syd Castle, however, was not too impressed with the situation, thinking that a man of Les's position should be driving and maybe was overlooking the amount of time he could save by travelling by car, too. Castle owned the well-known Castle Brothers Haulage company located behind the Kop (also known then as the North Stand or Gelderd End) as well as the United Garage on Elland Road, a half-brick's throw from the stadium gates. Dave Cocker said, 'Around

1964 and my dad's still walking, he wasn't bothered about having a car. Syd advised him to get a car and eventually told him he had a great one that he could have for nothing; it looked a bit ratty but otherwise it was perfectly fine.' The manufacturer is a mystery, but Dave recalled it as a proper banger, 'This was pre-season – my dad accepted the car and parked it in the stadium tunnel area near the corner between the West Stand and the Kop so he could paint it as there was lighting in the tunnel. The tunnel area was near where all the ground-staff equipment was stored as well. Everything. So he got some paint and hand-painted it himself under the electric lights in what he thought was a lovely shade of green, but when he saw it in the real light it looked bloody horrible. Syd was even more unimpressed now to the extent that he demanded the car back!'

Les's crowded work calendar included six England under-23 fixtures up to the end of May 1964. On 13 November 1963, the team drew 1-1 with Wales at Bristol City's Ashton Gate. Leeds' Gary Sprake kept goal for Wales. Two weeks later, the England team hammered the West Germans 4-1 at Liverpool's Anfield, without Les however, as he was on club duty at Maine Road where Manchester City were beating Leeds in the League Cup. On 5 February 1964 England beat Scotland 3-2 at Newcastle United's St James' Park. Nearly 35,000 attended and Billy Bremner played for Scotland. In Rouen, France, on 8 April, Leeds' Paul Reaney made his England under-23 debut at right-back in a 2-2 draw.

By then, Dr Neil Phillips, 31, from Wales, working with Middlesbrough at the time, had joined the under-23s set-up, invited by Walter Winterbottom. Alf Ramsey made the arrangement more official late April 1964, asking him to be the team's physician. Early in their friendship, Ramsey advised Dr Phillips, 'We don't do this job for the money, we do it for the love of the game and the players,' and the medic wholeheartedly agreed.

Soon after the close of the 1963/64 season, the England under-23s were on tour and had friendlies in Hungary, Israel and Turkey. The senior squad, meanwhile, had a tour of South America to undertake. Joe Mercer was the under-23s' manager at the time but had been ordered to rest for the good of his health, having endured a torrid season with Aston Villa and narrowly avoiding relegation from the First Division. He was replaced by Sheffield United manager John Harris, a Scot, which meant Les was the only Englishman involved in the running of the under-23s. The tour matches started in Budapest on 13 May, a 2-1 defeat to Hungary, followed four days later by a 4-0 win over Israel in Tel Aviv. Their final match was against Turkey, a 3-0 defeat in Istanbul. Due to dates clashing, Les was forced to miss Leeds' friendlies in a tour of East Germany, including a 3-1 defeat against an East German Olympic XI in Berlin, allegedly watched by 60,000.

In his exceptional autobiography *Doctor to the World Champions*, Dr Phillips wrote about the tour and his time working with Les. He described how, before the Hungary fixture, a Russian army officer had given them a guided tour of Budapest even though it was the Hungarian Football Association's affair. He told them that the city's bridges were voluntarily rebuilt by Hungarian citizens, plus there was a statue of Russian soldiers supporting a figure holding an olive leaf, intimating that Russia's presence (or rule) there was welcomed. Talking with Phillips, one Hungarian FA official contradicted the story, stating that the Russians had a different interpretation of the word 'voluntary' to that of the Hungarians. 'When the war ended, all the bridges needed to be rebuilt. At the end of each working day, all the able-bodied people of Budapest were ordered to report to the bridges. They worked on rebuilding them until sunset. No one was paid. Because no one was paid, the Russians deemed it as voluntary labour.'

Despite the match being played in 100 degrees-plus temperatures in the Tel-Aviv stadium, England coped well with the extreme heat and overzealous challenges from opposing players to easily beat Israel 4-0. Apart from several bruises there were no serious injuries. After the game we all attended another formal banquet provided by the Israeli FA. It was another late night and I found, as did the players, these post-match affairs tedious, especially the long speeches by the various officials.

'Most unusually, when on an England tour, the day after was a free day. Most of the players decided on a day at the beach, Les Cocker and I decided on a visit to Jerusalem. The Israelis provided us with a taxi. Unbeknown to us, the road journey involved travelling along the Road of Courage, so named in memory of all the Israelis who had been killed building this road to Jerusalem. It was regarded as very dangerous, with travellers on occasion subject to sniper gunfire. The driver travelled at alarming speed, sometimes over 100 mph.' He then described climbing the steps of The Citadel ('well worth it'), and later, an Israeli official inviting he and Les up some stairs to a securely locked room, advising that it was believed by some to be the room where the Last Supper was held. The room was tiny, nothing like the painting, with a small brick altar on one side of the room and a cylindrical stone pillar, but otherwise bare.

Alf Ramsey was single-minded in the planning for his England side, he knew the changes required and he knew how he would implement them. He was not interested at all in the views of men who had never played at professional level or coached or managed teams. This disdain certainly applied to the FA hierarchy and to the press who, in modern parlance, he regarded as toxic.

That corners routine

Les often attended coaching seminars, his 'secondary employers' the Football Association in attendance too to provide some or other lecture on how the game 'should' be played. Les would tell son Dave of his exasperation at some of the guidance and directives the FA preached. One such hot topic was the 'correct' way of taking corners during matches. Les, putting on a posh voice, would explain how corners should proceed (according to the FA), 'At a corner, the attacking players shall stand on the 18-yard box and the defending players shall stand on the six-yard box. The player who takes the corner kick will strike the ball into the penalty area in the proximity of the penalty spot where the defending goalkeeper will attempt to catch the ball. And that is how a corner kick should be defended.'

Very few goals were ever scored from corners, it just wasn't done – the attacking players would rush in like a cavalry and the defenders would either stand still or rush out towards those attackers. The football would usually end up in the middle of the penalty area with the practically unchallenged keeper catching it – and if he was challenged, he would bring his knee up mid-jump to knock the opposing player out of the way. And there was one defender standing on the goal line inside the front post and one inside the back post. All in all, corners were a pointless tradition, like baubles on Christmas trees or FA selection committees.

But it gave Les an idea which he relayed to Revie, suggesting they try something new for corners in training. Utilising Jack Charlton, by now an England international, Revie and Les instructed him to stand inside the near post to the corner, with his arms in the air, while goalkeeper Gary Sprake was instructed to try and defend the kick once the ball came over. Importantly, the ball was to be pinpointed (or 'pinged' in modern parlance) to Charlton's head by dead-ball experts, John Giles or Peter Lorimer (and, later, Eddie Gray). With the exclusion of Sprake, the players devised a few signals so as to indicate what kind of cross the taker planned to put in. Sprake was told to try and deal with the cross but now Charlton was in front of him, obscuring his view of the ball's trajectory as well.

Sprake soon realised he was virtually incapable of stopping a goal and he didn't know what to do to deal with the threat. He couldn't push Charlton out of the way or barge through him as it would be a foul. Most of the time, Charlton did not even need to jump for the ball, the accuracy was so good. Revie decided to put the plan into action in matches, and it worked a treat. It was to prove a very unpopular development, a paradigm shift, in football. And later, Ramsey's England would employ the same idea.

4

1965 – on the up

TO COMMEMORATE Leeds United's promotion to the First Division, singer and United fan Ronnie Hilton recorded a single with some of the Leeds players, titled 'Leeds United Calypso' and backed with 'Elland Road Baht'at'. It came out in late May 1964 but had little impact on the pop charts, one review saying that the track was a half-hearted attempt at a calypso but unfortunately their singing wasn't as good as their playing.

Also in the world of entertainment, Britain witnessed the arrival of what would become a football if not cultural institution: the premiere series of *Match of the Day* was aired on BBC Two, from Saturday 22 August 1964, to mark the start of the 1964/65 season. It was transmitted at 6.30pm with the audience reported to be just 20,000. BBC Two had only been in existence for four months and audience reach was severely limited for a while; it would be a few years before managers were able to get back home in time to watch the highlights programme and then telephone each other to discuss their afternoon, like Don Revie and Bill Shankly famously did.

When Les Cocker returned home on late Saturday nights after a Leeds match, he would sit quietly and recall the events to himself, writing down detailed observations of how each player had performed, noting what they had done well and, more importantly, any aspects they needed to improve. This would even extend to opposing teams and individual players. He would use the 1960s compilation vinyl LP *The Hit Makers* to rest on. Dave still has the record and the ink-marked sleeve from Les's favourite fountain pen. Les was a big fan of pop music from that era.

1964/65

The previous season had been an excellent success for Leeds, promoted as champions. This season would see a quite incredible amount of pressure placed upon the club personnel, and Les had his England under-23 commitments to take into account too. The Beatles' 'Eight Days a Week', released in late 1964, could so easily have applied to his work situation. And his commitments would only get heavier as Leeds marched on and Ramsey's England made preparations for the 1966 World Cup to be held in their own country.

Don Revie, before the start of the 1964/65 campaign, declared his intention of giving those players who had impressed so much the previous term a run in the First Division; he believed they would not disappoint. This was particularly good news for those young players who had proved integral in the team's dramatic ascendancy, specifically Norman Hunter who played in every league game, and Gary Sprake and Paul Reaney who missed just two games between them. Revie's confidence in his young charges was also testament to his trust in the work of Syd Owen and Les, bringing youths through the ranks and preparing them supremely well for the big step up to first-team football. There was no such thing as an easy game or mere walk in the park when it came to Second Division football, and the top division would only be tougher. In addition to that trio of 'young uns', and the 'old hand' of Billy Bremner (not yet 22), other young players such as Terry Cooper, Jimmy Greenhoff, Paul Madeley and 'the Cannonball Kid' Peter Lorimer, Leeds' youngest-ever debutant, had enjoyed run-outs in the first 11.

One youngster of whom great things were anticipated was Eddie Gray, but his first-team debut had to be put on hold due to injury in a reserve match against Sheffield Wednesday. The injury itself – a muscle tear in his left thigh – did not seem overly serious at first, and with good intentions, naturally, Les worked with Gray to help a swift recovery. Things did not go quite to how Les had planned them. From Eddie's autobiography, 'One day, at 9.30 in the morning, Les told me to sit in a hot herbal salt bath and not get out until he told me to do so. Unfortunately, he forgot about me – equally unfortunately, I did not have the good sense to realise this. I had been in that bath for around two hours before Les gave me the nod to get out, and by that time, certain parts of my body felt like they were on fire.' For any readers of a more sensitive nature, please skip the next line. Eddie was referring to his testicles, adding that he was 'walking like John Wayne' for a while afterwards.

In terms of on-field accomplishments, Leeds' promotion-winning season of 1963/64 took some topping, but 1964/65 probably achieved the feat. The less-than-angelic upstarts of Elland Road were not only battling it out with the devils of Old Trafford for the league championship title but also contested two epic battles with them in the FA Cup semi-final. Manchester United would triumph in the league, finishing top by way of goal average over the 42 matches, while Leeds would win in the FA Cup to reach Wembley for the first time in their history. April 1965 was a most hectic of months for the club and for Les. Leeds had to play eight league games, including three in four days, and Les was on England duty on 7 April too, for the under-23s against Czechoslovakia at Elland Road.

The Wembley pitch was known for its grass being thick and lush. All well and good to look at but not so great to play on as it would sap a player's energy. In the run-up to the Leeds v Liverpool FA Cup Final, Les opined that the Leeds players should train on a similar surface to that of Wembley's. Such a place existed just a short distance from Les's home, and Elland Road – Farnley Park in Leeds 12. Alas, for Leeds and their followers, the final seemed to overwhelm the players somewhat, and the Wembley pitch sapped their energy more quickly than anticipated. Not helping matters was the game going into 30 minutes of extra time. It wasn't a great match, in truth, Leeds' highlight being Bremner's perfectly struck half-volley to level the scores, but overall Liverpool shaded it 2-1 and won the FA Cup for the first time.

The matter of transfers in English football in the 1960s is an interesting one, a time when players did not have agents, whereas nowadays it feels like even the agents have agents. If one club wanted to buy a registered player, the protocol was that they should approach the club holding his registration to enquire of his availability. If a non-attached player, such as a schoolboy, was being sought after then it was often a club's scout who started negotiations. 'Sweeteners', probably better known as 'bungs', to young players' parents were common, and Leeds undoubtedly were involved in such affairs, almost certainly like every big club in the British Isles. With respect to the absence of agents, some footballers were fortunate to have family members advising them and looking after their interests. One prominent player who Leeds were known to be interested in was represented by his father, who himself was known to require money before he would allow the club to speak with his son. Revie would be castigated for this in later years, but the truth was, he was one of many working like this. Speaking of illegal approaches and the like, it was reported that Leeds-registered Jim McCalliog was signed 'illegally' for Chelsea from the club in 1963.

During the close season, England under-23s had a trio of matches on the continent, versus West Germany,

1965 – ON THE UP

Czechoslovakia and Austria. Plenty of incident and controversy abound, and Ken Jones of the *Daily Mirror* reported as England lost 1-0 to the Germans on 25 May 1965, a game in which Alan Ball was booked for kicking the ball away in anger when disputing a refereeing decision, 'In an explosive start to their three-match tour, Young England were involved in angry incidents that spread finally to the touchline in the second half. As trainer Les Cocker of Leeds was about to run on to give right-half Tommy Smith treatment, he was pulled back by an official crowd steward. The steward was removed at team manager Alf Ramsey's request. Ramsey said afterwards, "Les Cocker was assaulted by the official and I asked the Germans to take the man away. I thought we were unlucky to begin the tour with a defeat."'

Former Leeds player John Stiles, son of Nobby, later told another story from that same defeat, involving his dad and, again, Les. It was a fiery match, the sort Nobby relished, with hard challenges and fouls aplenty, and Les had been kept busy attending to various injuries throughout. One recipient of medical attention – probably just cold water and a 'magic' sponge – was Nobby. He had been 'clattered' in one challenge without seeing which player had hit him, partly because Nobby was very short-sighted but also because the challenge was from behind. He asked Les to identify the culprit. Les ignored the question, instead telling Stiles to forget about it and just 'concentrate on your game'. Shortly afterwards, the same German player hit Stiles again with another excessive tackle, though Nobby wasn't in need of treatment this time. He was the next time, however, after ending up in a heap on the touchline, but again he hadn't seen who his aggressor had been. 'Les, who was it?' he asked again while receiving treatment. Les told him to not worry about it and to get on with the game. 'But it was their number four,' he added as he exited the scene. Retribution exacted by Nobby Stiles soon followed.

Matters did not improve for Alan Ball in the final match, in Austria, and Les was involved again, too. On Wednesday, 2 June 1965 in Vienna, Austria's under-23s hosted their England counterparts. Ball was sent off in England's second 0-0 draw within a week. 'Tearfully, and with the consoling arm of trainer Les Cocker around him, he was banned after 60 minutes, paying the price for another flash of temper,' it was reported. Already booked, he had thrown the ball at the referee, Hungarian Gyula Gere, for not allowing him to take a free kick quickly. England chief Alf Ramsey told the press that he could not comment on the incident. If he had done, it would most likely have got him into trouble.

Ball was a firebrand of a footballer, a flame-haired fighter for the cause, and playing for England was his proudest passion. He was a rare talent, a young man who would never give up the fight. Those incidents of indiscipline, though, were seen as a serious threat to his England career. Regardless of the overzealousness of both referees, any bookings and dismissals were always condemned by members of the English media and the Football Association. Ramsey would entertain no such thing but there was no getting away from the issue, Ball needed to improve his temperament if he wanted to play in the World Cup finals the following year.

In Les, Ramsey saw a former player with less talent than Ball but similar attitude and disposition. To Ramsey, Les's 'consoling arm' around Ball's shoulders after the player had been dismissed signified more than just comradely comforting, it showed that he would influence, for the better, the player's future conduct. Probably to the surprise of no one involved with professional football in England, Ramsey 'promoted' Les to the position of trainer for the senior squad. In other words, Les would be prominently involved in the World Cup finals of 1966. No one can have doubted he deserved it.

Harold Shepherdson

Already with Ramsey was a Middlesbrough man called Harold Shepherdson. As a player, Shepherdson was a centre-half, commanding and capable, but he was forced to retire at 28 due to a knee injury sustained while on an FA coaching course. Before the retirement, he served in World War Two as an army staff sergeant physical training instructor while still occasionally appearing for Middlesbrough. He was taken on as assistant trainer and moved up to be the club's trainer in 1949. His work impressed England officials and in 1957 he became trainer to the national side under Walter Winterbottom.

Les, who had seen his club finish as runners-up in the 1965 First Division title race and the FA Cup Final, was probably not too disappointed to learn that he had not claimed the Pipe Smoker of the Year award either. Prime minister Harold Wilson 'won' it, though it is doubtful anyone was consciously competing for the title. Dave Cocker believes his dad finished third for the honour. A bit of vague and smoky trivia for you there. Revie had banned Leeds players from smoking yet was it often the case on the team coach to matches that the manager himself would light up a cigar and Les would smoke a pipe. There were always rumours of certain Leeds players – an Englishman, a Welshman and a Scotsman – frequently flouting the ban, and it's entirely possible that their misbehaviour occurred on the same coach journeys, the smoke blending with the aromas of cigar and tobacco pipe from the front seats.

In 1965 came the formation of the Variety Club of Great Britain Golf Society, itself a part of the famed charitable organisation the Royal Variety Club (now named Variety, the Children's Charity) which had been around for considerably longer, raising funds for the benefit of disabled and disadvantaged children and young people. The golf society was formed to continue such wonderful work, and charity golfing events have been organised ever since, involving professional and amateur golfers as well as famous people from football and other sports, film, TV, stage, pop music, and so on. Les, like many colleagues in professional football, was an avid golfer and played regularly despite his busy schedule. Some things never change in life regardless of age, such as football men loving competition in just about everything, and playing golf was a perfect opportunity to show this. Leeds players and staff would have a golf day every week, taken seriously by those adept at the sport.

The Variety's golf society organised many pro-celebrity tournaments for their fundraising, Les and Revie often taking part. There cannot be many more pleasurable ways of helping and doing good for society than raising money by playing a game you love with friends and famous colleagues. Les would enjoy friendships through golf with many celebrities, including Sean Connery, Bruce Forsyth, Jimmy Tarbuck and Val Doonican, to name just a few. There was also a moderately famous film actor/wrestler who had been an Olympic weightlifter too, who liked to play golf, named Harold Sakata, probably better known as Oddjob from the James Bond classic *Goldfinger*. Before being hired, Sakata was part of a wrestling tour which had taken in various towns and cities across the country, including Leeds, a maybe surprising hotbed for professional wrestling, thanks in large part to the sterling work of George de Relwyskow Junior, another man with a fascinating history who deserves a separate book to be written about him. George had been a fine wrestler himself but moved into promoting bouts after retiring from the sport due to injuries sustained during World War Two. His father, George senior, had been an Olympic medal-winning wrestler in 1908; professional wrestling was then often promoted as a variety act in theatres and music halls, and his fame spread rapidly. George junior, based in Oakwood, Leeds, was a friend of the Cocker family and, naturally, knew Sakata too. It was George who kindly set up a golf match between Dave Cocker and Sakata at Sand Moor Golf Club, when Sakata had been in the region on a wrestling tour. Dave was too 'star struck' to remember whether it was he or Oddjob who won the match.

Probably Les's best friend with whom he regularly golfed with was ex-Leeds and Wales player Harold Williams, another small man with a big heart and lots of pals. Williams was always full of good-natured mischief, a regular 'target' being John Charles before he left for Juventus in 1957. Just as an example, it had been Williams who, on a Hull to Rotterdam ferry, once 'made' Charles seek out the ship's captain to ask where the billiards table was.

And now, with no connection at all to the Variety Club golf society's formation, I can share the info that I too was born in 1965. I have never played a full round of golf in my life, though I did, and this is a true story folks, to the amazement of my three opponents, hit a 50-yard hole-in-one on a mini-golf course in Great Yarmouth, circa 1983.

5

1966, England's glory

1965/66

Was the previous season a one-off or could Leeds emulate or, even, surpass it? In certain respects, the answer was a firm no, for their FA Cup hopes ended in the fourth round at Chelsea and the First Division championship wasn't as close this time. In spite of being resident in the top six all season, it never looked likely that they would finish top. Leeds came second again, runners-up to Liverpool by six points and above third-placed Burnley by merit of a better goal average.

The 1965/66 season was, though, their European debut, and they gave it a right good go, as West Yorkshire folk might have put it. Thousands more miles were added to the personal mileometers of Leeds' players and staff. And as an obvious consequence, they were able to spend even less time with their loved ones. Naturally, such 'hazards' of the job could be detrimental to relationships, and that old adage absence makes the heart grow fonder would be frequently put to the test. These new European assignments demonstrated that the more success a club achieved, the more it might suffer. And Les Cocker's season would be even busier than the players' due to his England duties, though just three under-23 fixtures were scheduled, and all in England. Alf Ramsey's priority was, indubitably, selecting and organising his senior squad and personnel for their 1966 World Cup crusade, with Les an integral part of those plans.

Les was featured, along with his favourite teapot (of all things!), in the *Daily Mirror* in late January 1966, the newspaper reporting, 'Presenting the world's most travelled teapot. It is the proud property of Les Cocker, Leeds United's trainer, and is always the first thing he packs for trips abroad. It has seen service in 12 different countries including Turkey, Switzerland and East Germany. Says Cocker, "I love a nice strong cuppa, and the only way to get one abroad is to make your own."' With Leeds' European travels as well as overseas matches for England in 1966 before the tournament, the teapot had many more excursions in store. During 1965/66, England had fixtures in Spain, Scotland, Finland, Norway, Denmark and Poland while Leeds' European assignments took in Italy, East Germany, Spain (twice) and Hungary.

Leeds' first foray into European football took place in the Inter-Cities Fairs Cup, each round consisting of two legs. Their first opponents were Torino, the Italian team from Turin, where Juventus were also based, in northern Italy.

In an attempt to confuse the Italian team for the first leg of the first round, at home, Don Revie decided to rearrange his players' shirt numbers, so Alan Peacock was number seven instead of his customary nine, for example. Billy Bremner became Leeds' first scorer in European football, a well-struck but speculative shot mishandled by goalkeeper Vieri. Soon after the match, Jack Charlton, Norman Hunter and Alan Peacock boarded a flight to London to join up with the full England squad for the match against Gary Sprake's Wales on the Saturday. Les would join them a little later. The second leg in the Torino tie was scheduled to kick off at 9.30pm GMT the following Wednesday, so Revie and Les arranged special late-night training sessions on the Sunday and Monday to try and acclimatise his team to the idea. They would also play with a spotted football to correspond with the 'European design' ball that would be used in Turin.

Thanks to a superbly resilient display of defending and counter-attacking, the 0-0 scoreline in Italy saw Leeds deservedly go through to the next round. The match, however, was more memorable due to a horrific challenge on Bobby Collins which put him out of the match – and out of football for a long time – as well as effectively ending his Leeds career, too. The 'cruel tackle', as some in the media described it, wasn't a tackle at all but an assault – Torino full-back Fabrizio Poletti had been nowhere near the ball when he deliberately ran into Collins at full pelt, kneeing him in the upper leg with such force that he broke the captain's thigh bone. Leeds' Willie

Bell, not in the side on the night, accompanied Collins in the ambulance to the hospital. Les and club secretary Cyril Williamson stayed nearby overnight while the rest of the contingent returned home. Collins would remain in Turin for two weeks. On his return to Elland Road, his rehabilitation, under Dr Ian Adams and Les Cocker, commenced. Les's Treatment of Injuries training course was being put to good use.

In the same month as Collins's injury, centre-forward Alan Peacock spoke of his own experiences of serious injury in a Sunday tabloid, as well as the 'whispers' suggesting Collins would never play again. Peacock had been in a similar situation, where many were writing him off, although he was back playing for not just Leeds but England within six months of an injury which had occurred in a collision with the East German Olympic XI keeper in the May 1964 friendly match in Berlin. He had a month in plaster and seemed to be recovering well, only for it to happen again in a pre-1964/65 season friendly in Northern Ireland. 'Leeds trainer Les Cocker, one of the best in the business, attended to me and, under his manipulation, the strength came back to that leg. Everything felt normal again,' Peacock wrote.

But then it went again in a practice match, meaning more time out trying to recuperate. It went again on his return to training. A specialist suggested another exploratory operation. 'It meant opening up the back of my leg from the thigh down to the calf muscle, and it was then they found what was causing the leg to collapse. A piece of gristle had mysteriously become detached and was floating around the muscles in the back of the leg. Every so often it stuck, and I lost all the power. A month went by after that op before the specialist said I could even think of training again ... Muscles wasted by ops and inactivity had to be rebuilt. Les Cocker devised special exercises and I had to shift, with my legs, weights heavier than I could ever have picked up with my arms. I had to do 12 laps round the track – a good three miles – every day. And at one stage I was running not only round the track but round the ground too.

For the second round of the Fairs Cup, East German opponents Leipzig were located behind the Iron Curtain and under Communist rule. Revie did not savour the prospect of Eastern Bloc hospitality and so ensured the club took their own food and the services of their own chef for the first leg, away on 24 November. Anywhere under Russian control must have felt cold and uninviting anyway, but the match was played on six inches of packed snow and possibly witnessed the first time the Leeds players wore boots with the studs filed down to expose the boot nails underneath, temporarily concealed by cardboard creations which lasted mere minutes, just long enough for the match officials to have checked, as was the rule. That was likely to have been Les's idea, though the reason seems to have changed for dramatic means over the years. Also, for better visibility during the match the pitch markings were painted in blue and an orange football used.

Peter Lorimer scored Leeds' first away goal in Europe, a low strike late in the match. Bremner headed in a second soon after, with Leipzig pulling a goal back to make it 2-1 to Leeds and all to play for. The Elland Road leg one week later ended as a 0-0 draw, enabling Leeds to progress to the third round. There, they overcame Spanish side Valencia, 2-1 on aggregate, and in the fourth round they disposed of Hungarian greats Újpesti Dózsa, 5-2 on aggregate. Alas, Leeds' first European adventure was to end in the replayed semi-final at Elland Road against Real Zaragoza, the Spanish side winning 3-1 on the night but going on to lose to Barcelona in the final.

During May 1966, the last month of the domestic season, Leeds were up against Burnley in the league at Turf Moor. A very special guest was in attendance to be introduced to the two teams on the pitch prior to the 3pm kick-off, and Les was particularly delighted to meet him: Field Marshal Bernard Montgomery, 1st Viscount Montgomery of Alamein. This was an inspirational man who Les was proud to have fought with and who he considered as a real war hero and leader.

Earlier in the season, a league match against Northampton Town at Elland Road on 16 October 1965 was full of goals, with Leeds winning 6-1 to lift them to second in the table. It was also new signing Mike O'Grady's debut, playing on the left wing. The match referee was Ray Tinkler. During the first half, he had felt unwell with a headache and, at half-time, with Leeds leading 3-1 he asked Leeds medical officer Dr Ian Adams to examine him. Doc Adams obliged, naturally, and diagnosed Tinkler's problem as severe migraine, advising that he should not continue officiating the match. Tinkler refused to take the doctor's advice, insisting he would complete the second half. Not only was the decision potentially harmful to his own health, there would be doubt over certain future events, involving Tinkler, to conspire against Leeds.

In the second half against Northampton, Bremner was booked for 'dangerous play' by Tinkler. The booking was unwarranted in the opinion of secretary Cyril Williamson, a former referee himself, Dr Neil Phillips too was an important part of the England set-up, with Dr Alan Bass the senior doctor who later said, 'Bremner was pulled down from behind and there seemed absolutely no reason why he should have been cautioned.' It constituted Bremner's fourth booking of the season, meaning he would probably be suspended for a significant period by the FA. Revie probably did not help the situation by asking Tinkler after the match to not report the booking to the FA, but it was understandable nonetheless. Bremner followed protocol by appealing the caution and requesting a personal hearing with the FA's disciplinary committee; that would take place in Sheffield in January 1966.

With the hearing attended by Tinkler and one of the linesmen from the match, recorded as 'L. Birbeck', Leeds were represented by Bremner, Revie, Les and Williamson, armed with a written affidavit from Dr Adams too, stating his involvement in the events at the Northampton match, specifically the matter of Tinkler's migraine. Clearly, the club were treating the matter with utmost seriousness. Not that it worked, as Tinkler denied having the migraine. With the committee supporting his version of events, they were effectively branding Dr Adams's report as untrue. Thus, Bremner's appeal was dismissed, the booking would stand and he was ordered to pay the costs of the hearing, too. Outside, soon after the hearing had ended, Tinkler allegedly apologised to Bremner for lying, but he had decided that admitting his indiscretion to the FA was not an option. As to how the Leeds contingent responded needs little imagination really, though it is safe to say that Tinkler will not have taken kindly to their instructions. A referee making a genuine error was acceptable, but not a referee being dishonest.

For English football fans, excitement and anticipation grew and grew as spring and summer of 1966 progressed, leading up to the tournament of tournaments, the World Cup finals in England. Les had been 'upgraded' to Ramsey's so-called Council of War, working closely with Harold Shepherdson and Ramsey himself. Dr Neil Phillips as also an important part of the England set-up, with Dr Alan Bass was the senior doctor. Dr Phillips's main involvement was with the pre-tournament preparations at Lilleshall where the squad would spend two weeks carrying out extensive training. 'We worked on the most minute detail of the training programme,' Dr Phillips said, while Ramsey had stated that while England might not be the best football team in the competition, he wanted to ensure that they were the fittest. He also employed Manchester United's Wilf McGuinness to assist with the training.

One of those players present at Lilleshall in 1966 was George Cohen, with whom I had arranged an interview. For reasons that will soon become clear he was greatly relieved at just being present at the training camp, and still in Ramsey's plans. I must admit, I was a tad cautious when telephoning him. What if he turned out to be a lousy, grumpy interviewee who wasn't too keen about being interviewed for the millionth time by someone he'd never heard of and didn't *want* to hear of? I had Allan 'Sniffer' Clarke to thank for getting me the appointment but knowing Allan, the little I do, it could have all been a mischief at play. But this book is not about me, it's about Les Cocker, their friend, so I calmed my concerns and dialled his number on that vintage contraption called a landline telephone.

George's lovely wife Daphne first answered my call, and I heard her calling him to the phone. As soon as he responded to my introduction of 'Hello, Mister Cohen' with a friendly rebuke, 'Call me George, for Christ's sake!', I knew it was going to be all right. Better than all right, in fact; Cohen has been a football hero of mine for as long as I remember, even though I was only a year old in 1966. I'm sure there are many other football fans who adore the man without ever seeing him play. He's not a 'real' Cockney as he isn't from the capital's East End and wasn't born within hearing range of Bow Bells, but you would be hard-pushed to notice from his friendly, chipper London accent. I firstly asked him about his dealings with Les and from then on the conversation just flowed; perfect!

'Les Cocker was an outstanding man, as far as I'm concerned,' he said, before adding – and chuckling at the same time – 'Alf Ramsey seemed to put him in charge of me for some reason or other! Les made you train hard, he wouldn't let anybody slack, at all. I got on great with him and, in a way, I loved training with him, he was so good to work with, such a good trainer. And he knew what an individual needed, he was very good that way, spotting areas that a player might need to work on. As I say, he was a hard man, he wouldn't let anyone under his control slack. The same goes with Harold Shepherdson as well, of course. They were a good double working for Alf Ramsey, very good indeed.

'When you were training with England, you weren't allowed to get away with anything. He [Les] was good with it though, he had a good way about him, you know. He was demanding, yes, but would ease you into the training, let me just say that he was never over the top with it. He was hard but fair, and wouldn't stand for any rubbish from players. It was exactly what Alf wanted from him. Alf controlled the coaching, of course, and he'd say that we were picked for the work we did with our clubs but when we were with England we would have to do this, that or the other for the team as we were playing with different people. The little man did exactly what Alf wanted, you know, and I liked him very, very much indeed.'

I asked about his club career. 'I started with Fulham as a midfield player but there wasn't much future for me with that because of Johnny Haynes, I was never going to replace him – one of the greatest players I've ever seen. Fulham manager Dugald Livingstone came in 1956 and asked me if I'd ever thought of playing at full-back. I said no. "Well," he said, "it's easy, you've got some speed" – my main asset was that I could sprint – and he said he'd like to play me there. So that's how I became a full-back.'

I suggested that he'd done pretty well at it, and that I'd read him described as England's best-ever right-back. 'Well, thank you very much for saying that, it's very good of you. You've had some good full-backs at Leeds! Well listen, I tried, and did as I was told. Dugald had been a fine full-back in his playing days, and Fulham had had Joe Bacuzzi as well, a good old-time full-back who played for Fulham just after the war and for a long time after. They both taught me a great deal, and other things came into the game, like overlapping full-backs. I loved that, as being a bit quicker I could get down the wing. My crossing wasn't as good as it could have been though! Back in the early days, the wingers were speedy but the full-backs weren't. So I became a full-back and I must admit, it seemed a doddle at the time but, of course, things got more difficult as time went on.'

Back to the matter of Les. 'He'd watch you play in practice matches and would point out things that you weren't doing or perhaps had forgotten, but he'd never do it in the way of bawling you out. More *pointing* it out, just a reminder, you understand. And it worked, certainly that way worked for me, not being bawled out. Les was a great one for helping you.

Like coming up to you when you were walking off the pitch, pointing out what I could have done better, or reminding me to keep doing certain things. Always reassuring and urgent at the same time. That was his way and it always impressed me, always impressed me.'

Cohen's situation, prior to the tournament, became worryingly complicated due to his sustaining a serious injury playing against winger Harry Burrows of Stoke City. Burrows, in his follow-through after striking the football, inadvertently sliced through Cohen's bursa – a sac which supplies the synovial fluid that lubricates the joints – in his right knee. In his autobiography, George told of 'a nasty feeling to sit, a few months before the World Cup, on a football field and look at your somewhat re-arranged knee covered in blood'.

Over the subsequent years, probably every England player involved then has told of how tough the training regime at Lilleshall was, but actual complaints seem few and far between, if, indeed, there were any. Cohen joked that Lilleshall was worse than a prisoner of war camp but without a moat, and Nobby Stiles said it was the hardest training he'd ever done in his life. Alan Ball, in the *Football Post*, commented, 'The workouts we had at Lilleshall before the World Cup were fantastic. We would break into four groups and do four different kinds of work in one session. We would go from Harold Shepherdson to Les Cocker, Wilf McGuinness and Alf Ramsey, and each session in itself would be enough for a normal morning. Some of us thought that, on top of a hard season, it would tire us for competitive football but after a short rest following the session we would feel ready to crack iron bars with our teeth.'

And on Ramsey, McGuinness commented, 'The training was strong and physical for the end of the season. The players were all divided into groups and we passed on each group after 15 minutes of hard slog. Every group was trying to outdo the other in the circuits and in the ball work. It was punishing stuff but the players really took to it. By the end the players knew they were really fit. Alf wanted it that way. He wanted everyone to give everything. Les and Harold were ideal for what was needed. Les came from Leeds, bit of a hard man. Harold had been in the job since Walter Winterbottom's time, very experienced, well respected. I don't think Alf ever trusted Les as much as Harold. Harold was the best number two you could have in an organisation. He hated making decisions himself but if you told him to stand on his head three times a day he would do it for you. He would always carry out instructions to the letter. Les was much more confrontational, seeking to discuss things and argue his point.'

Ramsey may not have had too many friends in the media or the echelons of football administration, but the players were assuredly with him all the way, willing to work through pain barriers for him and England's cause. On a more personal note, Dagenham-born Ramsey's critics enjoyed the legend that he had taken elocution lessons to 'better himself'. When I asked Cohen about this, I could almost hear him shrug his shoulders,

'If it's true, we were never sure you see, then someone will have advised him early in the day that it might do him good. He was always all right with the people he met, that's what mattered to us. Besides, it doesn't do any harm, does it? Anyway, I greatly admired him, I must admit. He put me in the team after all!'

England's tournament began with a 0-0 draw against Uruguay on 11 July. The opening match was described as dreadful and the most arid of draws, and England's performance uninspiring. The Uruguayans were interested only in not losing, with minimal ambitions in attack. For their part in the turgid affair, England played poorly and made scant impression on Uruguay's solid defence. This had been the first time England had failed to score in a home match since 1938.

The following day, the England players and staff were treated to a leisurely visit to Pinewood Studios. There, among others, they met Sean Connery and watched him filming a scene on the next James Bond movie, *You Only Live Twice*. Film star Yul Brynner was also there, his thriller *The Double Man* also in production, mingling with the England group. It will all have been great fun for movie-mad Les, who loved his Bonds, as well as good war films, and virtually anything with Clint Eastwood or David Niven in. Connery enjoyed golf too, and the links, please excuse the pun, do not end there. But more of that later.

Five days after the Uruguay draw, England beat Mexico 2-0. Mexico were equally intent on avoiding defeat as Uruguay had been, and again England's form disappointed, but at least Bobby Charlton delivered, scoring once late in the first half with a screamer and effectively setting up Roger Hunt's decisive goal in the second.

Another win came four days later, 2-0 against France, but it was another disjointed and unconvincing display from England. Possibly the overriding memories of this match are of Jimmy Greaves suffering a nasty gash to his right shin, putting his tournament prospects in doubt, and a bad foul from Nobby Stiles which put his England future in doubt. Cohen told me, while laughing at the memory, 'I remember the foul Nobby made on the captain, Simon. I said, "Gawd, Jesus Christ, Nobby, why did you do it?" and he explained, "He called me Nor-bare!"' More laughter, from us both, then Cohen continued, 'Apparently, some in the FA wanted him out of the team after that. Alf was having none of that, of course. The fact is, Nobby was marvellous in front of me, he was absolutely bloody marvellous, and I had a good right-winger too, in Alan Ball. We had a good sort of triangle there, all part of Alf's plans.'

As a consequence of Stiles's foul, which put the Frenchman out of the game, there were calls from the media and FA for him to be dropped from the England team for the next match, against Argentina. Some even said he should never play for England again. In later years, Stiles commented that the foul had not been deliberate, adding, 'Everybody was saying that there was no way I should play against Argentina but Alf told me that I would play as long as I performed like I did against France for the first 70 minutes, not like the last 20 minutes. There was a lot of extra pressure on me then and I remember dear old Les Cocker and Harold Shepherdson taking me into the big bathroom at the dressing rooms at Wembley before the [Argentina] game. And they said you owe this fella something, keep your head no matter what. And I did, even though there was a lot of provocation.'

The calls from within the FA for Stiles to be excluded came from two officials. Ramsey disagreed and responded by telling them that if Stiles went then so would he. And if, by any chance Ramsey felt isolated in the drama, Les informed him that if 'they' succeeded in getting rid of Stiles then he would also leave his job in protest. There is little doubt that Shepherdson and McGuinness would have agreed with Les on the matter.

The quarter-final against Argentina ended in a 1-0 win on 23 July. It wasn't a spectacular game but certain Argentina individuals made spectacles of themselves. Before the players even lined up on the Wembley pitch, there were Argentines up to unsavoury things. Les witnessed some of their antics and would never forget them, particularly the sight of one player urinating in the Wembley tunnel and others trying to intimidate England players with sly little kicks and digs. The match itself descended into debacle at times, with occasional suggestions that a game of football might break out. The main culprit on the pitch was Argentina's captain and number ten, Antonio

Rattín, who seemed more interested in annoying the German referee, Rudolf Kreitlein, than playing football. Rattín was first cautioned around the 30th minute for tripping Bobby Charlton and then, a few minutes later, booked a second time and consequently dismissed. But he refused to go, as if expecting Kreitlein to relent and reverse his decision, until at last, slowly, reluctantly, he trudged off the pitch and around the circuit towards the tunnel, accompanied by his trainer. The whole fiasco took nearly ten minutes to end, while it was late in the second half before England notched the vital goal, Geoff Hurst with a perfect glancing header from a Martin Peters cross.

Cohen said, 'They certainly gave us a good bashing, including one of our officials! Their captain tried to run the whole competition. And the referee in our match against them was getting a bit mad, you know. They were trying to goad him all the time. In the end, Rattín had to go, he really had to go. I was pleased, he was a bloody good player! It was a hard game and I thought we did well to beat them.' Immediately after the final whistle, the whole world could see Cohen about to swap shirts with Alberto González only for Ramsey to angrily intervene and prevent the exchange. England's left-back, Ray Wilson, can't have been paying attention as he happily swapped his own shirt with González almost straightaway.

Post-match, back in the dressing-rooms area, some Argentina players tried to kick the England door in. It was reported that Ramsey asked Les what they should do, and Les replied, 'Let them in if they want to come in!' And Jack

Charlton, close by, agreed, as did Wilson who said, 'For Christ's sake, let em in,' emboldened by the fact that 'half a dozen of them were smaller than me'. Les walked to the door, opened it and, with Jack looming behind him, said, 'Do you want to come in?' The Argentine players declined the invitation and stopped the commotion.

Interviewed after the match, Ramsey caused more bad feeling when saying, 'It seemed a pity so much Argentinian talent is wasted. Our best football will come against the right type of opposition – a team who come to play football, and not act as animals.' He was never forgiven for the 'animals' remark, certainly not in Argentina anyway, while the match was christened *'El Robo del Siglo'* ('The Robbery of the Century') there.

The semi-final came on 26 July and produced a Bobby Charlton-inspired 2-1 victory over Portugal, his best game of the tournament, and a match without controversy. The opening goal was a straightforward (for a man of his talent, at least) shot, driven into the net from just outside the Portugal penalty area after a Hunt effort had been blocked and the ball had spun out to the quick-witted, fleet-footed Charlton. England failed to build on the goal or their dominance and the scoreline remained the same. For too long it became a nervy affair and Portugal pressed for the equaliser. Thankfully, England's goalkeeper Gordon Banks, and back four of Cohen, Jack Charlton, Bobby Moore and Wilson, superbly supported by the unstoppable Stiles, held firm. And, 11 minutes from time England scored again, Hunt pulling the ball back for Charlton to strike sweetly from near the edge of the area. It wasn't over yet though, a few minutes later came a penalty for Portugal after Jack Charlton had swiped the ball away from the goal with his hand after a Torres header had beaten Banks. Eusébio scored the penalty to make it 2-1 but England held out to reach the final.

In the days leading up to the showpiece, skipper Bobby Moore was a major doubt after coming down with tonsillitis. Ramsey considered the possibility of Moore's absence, asking Les and Shepherdson if they felt his understudy Norman Hunter would fare as a replacement if Moore was too ill to play. Les, unsurprisingly as he knew everything there was to know about his Leeds colleague, expressed his complete confidence in Hunter if called into action.

Innumerable reports, opinions and anecdotes have been put to paper since 30 July and the 1966 World Cup Final, so there are probably no more revelations left. The match itself was an exciting, 'end to end', energy-sapping epic, strewn with errors but a glorious battle between two fine sides. It proved to be a perfect finale to the competition. West Germany opened the scoring on 12 minutes, a low, angled drive from Helmut Haller latching on to a mistimed headed clearance from Wilson. In the 18th minute, Wolfgang Overath fouled Moore in the Germans' half and Moore took the free kick quickly, perfectly floating the ball to Hurst who headed home sharply to make it 1-1. The scoreline stayed that way for over half an hour into the second half until, in the 77th minute, a Hurst shot was only partially cleared by the German defence, the ball looping into the penalty area where Peters finished with a superb half-volley. West Germany pressed for an equaliser in the closing moments and in the 89th minute were fortunate to be awarded a free kick after the referee, Gottfried Dienst, adjudged Jack Charlton to have fouled Uwe Seeler as they challenged a header. The resultant kick caused mayhem in the penalty area and the ball was deflected across the England six-yard box, wrong-footing the England defence and allowing Wolfgang Weber to snatch the equaliser and make it 2–2. For the first time in a World Cup Final, the match went into extra time.

It had been a well-fought contest so far, played in good spirit and without controversy. That would all go out of the figurative window, however, during the extra 30 minutes. Eleven minutes into the first period, Ball struck a low cross into the Germans which was received by Hurst around seven yards from goal. Hurst swivelled brilliantly and hit a terrific shot, the ball hitting the underside of the crossbar, bouncing down to be immediately cleared by a defender. The nearest England man to the goal was Hunt, who celebrated, convinced that Hurst had scored, but the referee wasn't sure – had the ball crossed the line? He walked across to the touchline to ask his linesman, Tofiq Bahramov from Azerbaijan in the USSR, who stated that it had indeed crossed the line, and so the Swiss referee awarded the goal, making the score 3-2 to England. One minute before the end of play, with West Germany desperately seeking to level again, Moore collected the ball and, with his right foot, struck a long pass to the unmarked Hurst, who drove forward for a few yards before thumping a fabulous shot on goal, straight to the top corner of Hans Tilkowski's net to complete a historic hat-trick and sealing the World Cup for his country.

Cohen said, 'I was too far away to see if the third goal went in; I met the goalkeeper [Tilkowski] once some years later and he said, "It did not go in!" smiling as he said it, and I just smiled back. In the end, we got another goal after that one, and that's what matters. I think we were a well-schooled side, otherwise we wouldn't have beaten the Germans.'

The whole of the ball perhaps did not cross the line and the Germans justifiably felt aggrieved that the goal stood. That said, the free kick against Jack Charlton which led to the Germans' equaliser should not have been awarded as it wasn't a foul, and Hurst added the fourth England goal anyway.

Scenes following the referee's full-time whistle showed players reacting differently, most delirious with joy but others, like Bobby Charlton, in tears, while brother Jack had dropped to his knees on the Wembley turf, emotional and perhaps exasperated and near-exhausted. Like most of the England personnel, Les celebrated on the pitch, joyfully embracing Ball and the front-toothless Stiles, who unforgettably would soon be skipping happily around the pitch with his team-mates parading the golden Jules Rimet Trophy.

That evening, at the Royal Garden Hotel in London, which incidentally had been the venue for the World Cup groups draw back in January, a reception was held in honour of the England team and personnel. Dr Phillips attended, recalling, 'The team made several balcony appearances during the evening. On one occasion, the wives joined us for our balcony appearance. Not to be outdone, prime minister Harold Wilson joined us. In order to gain entrance to the balcony, my wife Margaret, observing protocol, allowed him to precede her through the small opening on to the balcony. He got stuck and so I witnessed my wife helping Harold Wilson on to the balcony by pushing with both hands, on his buttocks!'

Afterwards, as Ramsey had given the England contingent a list of nightclubs and restaurants where they would be made most welcome, players and personnel dispersed to venues of their choosing. Dr Phillips wrote, 'Inevitably, Les Cocker and I gravitated together, as we were great friends having worked consistently together with the under-23 team during the previous three years. Les, his wife Nora, Margaret and I opted to visit the Bunny Club in Park Lane as their guests.' There, they needed nothing to eat and declined the free champagne too, with Phillips saying that he wanted to remember every moment of the day, and did not want to wake up in the morning through a haze of alcoholic stupor as the memories of the day must 'remain clear in his mind forever'. Les agreed wholeheartedly. Dr Phillips closed with, 'We chatted through every kick of the final. We reminisced about our experiences during the past three years. We drank squash all night, our wives enjoyed the champagne. Our conversation was so intense that we missed the arrival of Ray Wilson and Bobby Charlton with their wives. Ray's presence was soon noticed by everyone however. As the cabaret came to a close, Ray mounted the stage and gave an excellent rendition of Al Jolson songs!'

Cohen told me some more about the day and the aftermath, 'Do you know, the FA made an awful lot of money out of the World Cup? After the end of the game, the final, Bobby Moore was called to one side, given some news to tell us all – "The FA have awarded us 22,000 quid."' George laughed again as he spoke to me, 'I immediately thought to myself, excited, "Jesus Christ, I'm rich!" and I then realised it was £1,000 each for the players in the squad. There was never any question, we were going to share the money equally between all the players, whether or not they played in the final. That is how strong the bond was between us all. They, the FA, made half a million quid from the World Cup. Half a million!

'But anyway, very fortunately, I saw Harold Wilson after the match, the prime minister, and he said, "You will not be paying any tax on your bonus." Well I thought that was marvellous, but it wasn't very much really. The Germans got a lot more money than that, I believe. There were other things too that really annoyed me – the fact that at the official dinner afterwards, the players' wives were not allowed to be with us at the dinner. I was shocked, you know. I thought it was gross bad manners, and I used to get on with some of those guys in the FA. It was gross, I mean, who would do such a thing?'

Les also received a £1,000 winning bonus and used it to buy a new Vauxhall Viva for himself and the family. Dave Cocker remembers it had the registration plate of GUG379D. Possibly not even remarked upon at the time, but while the 11 players in the England side in the final received a winner's medal, the rest of the squad and the training staff, even the manager, did not.

Months after the final, Les was interviewed for a Leeds United yearbook, 'When Walter Winterbottom was the England team manager, I got my first chance to learn how things go at representative level, for I became trainer to the England under-23 side against Israel. Since then I've worked under Billy Wright, Joe Mercer and John Harris, and I've learnt something from every one of them. You never stop learning in this game. And one of the greatest honours to come my way was when Sir Alf Ramsey and Harold Shepherdson called on me to help them in preparing the England squad for the 1966 World Cup. That's something I'll never forget.'

6

1967 to 1970 – Leeds' time and turn for glory?

'YOU'LL GET paid for it, Les,' the prime minister, Harold Wilson, assured Les Cocker, having popped round for a cup of tea on his day off. They were discussing Gannex, a waterproof fabric invented by Joseph Kagan, of Kagan Textiles of Elland, West Yorkshire. Gannex raincoats consisted of an outer layer of nylon and an inner layer of wool with air between them. Kagan was a friend of Wilson, who first wore the distinctive raincoat in 1956 while on a world tour with the Labour Party; it caught media attention and became something of a fashion icon from then on. Dave Cocker remembers, a few years later, Wilson arriving in a beautiful, black Rover P5B, chauffeur-driven of course, at their home in Kirkdale Gardens. He only visited on Fridays, apparently. He would drink tea and have a few biscuits with Les and Nora, and he wanted to persuade Les to wear Gannex raincoats to help his friend's business. 'You'll get paid for it, Les, as well as a free Gannex raincoat.' The finer details are not known but Les did agree to the request. Dave added, 'I'd get home from school and there's Harold supping tea with my mum and dad, and I'm thinking, "Bloody hell, the prime minister's in our front room!" It's a shame he was a Huddersfield fan and not a Leeds fan, though.'

Leeds manager Don Revie was well known to be superstitious, an eccentric characteristic which perhaps betrayed his intelligence and his usual meticulousness and professionalism. Les was not superstitious at all but Revie's foibles did, in a manner of speaking, involve Dave. For instance, for Leeds away games, suited-up Dave would always travel down with a supporters' club coach and then meet his dad outside whichever stadium Leeds were to be playing in, as Les would have a match ticket for him. This was usually around an hour and a half before kick-off, and Dave would join the Leeds players in the changing room where Revie would usually ask him to nip out and buy him five Hamlet cigars. Dave would duly do so and if Leeds went on to win the match then that was a new ritual to adhere to, despite Dave always wondering what difference five Hamlets could actually make.

1966/67

Aside from the Second Division championship trophy, Leeds had yet to win any silverware under Revie. By now, the squad consisted in the main of internationally capped players at senior or youth level, plus of course they had a World Cup winner at centre-half in squad member Norman Hunter, as well as

1967 TO 1970 – LEEDS' TIME AND TURN FOR GLORY?

trainer Les. Their combined experience could only help the Leeds cause, it was surely just a matter of time, wasn't it? Well, perhaps, but success wouldn't be theirs this season.

In the league Leeds finished a creditable fourth, on 55 points, five fewer than champions Manchester United. In Europe, in the Inter-Cities Fairs Cup, the club's travels had taken them to the Netherlands, Spain, Italy, Scotland and Yugoslavia. They had beaten DWS Amsterdam, Valencia, Bologna and Kilmarnock to reach the two-legged final where they would be facing the renowned Dinamo Zagreb. The Yugoslavs were too strong for Leeds on home ground – a 2-0 defeat – the first time they had conceded more than one goal away in European competition. In the second leg, at Elland Road, Leeds battered Zagreb's defence but were lacking a real cutting edge up front, having to make do with a 0-0 draw.

In the FA Cup, having disposed of Crystal Palace and West Bromwich Albion comfortably, Leeds were drawn to play Sunderland at Roker Park in the fifth round. The teams drew 1-1, necessitating a replay at Elland Road four days later, Wednesday, 15 March 1967; it also ended 1-1 but is remembered more for other reasons. The official attendance was 57,892, a Leeds record, but in reality it was undoubtedly higher as scores more spectators gained entry thanks in part to the club's inability to make the match all-ticket due to lack of time to produce the tickets. Ten minutes in, a ten-foot crush barrier on the terraces near the corner of the Lowfields Road stand and the Scratching Shed collapsed. Referee Ray Tinkler halted the match while numerous spectators spilled beyond the perimeter track and on to the football pitch. Under the overall supervision of Dr Adams, the injured were treated by St John Ambulance Brigade nursing staff, and ambulances transported 18 people to the Leeds General Infirmary. Mercifully, there were no serious injuries reported; it could have been so much worse.

The tie's second replay was staged five nights later at Hull City's Boothferry Park. With extra time once more looking likely, Jimmy Greenhoff won a disputed penalty which John Giles scored from to win the match 2-1. Sunderland players angrily claimed Greenhoff was offside and that it was a dive anyway. Seconds after the restart, Terry Cooper was brought down by Sunderland's Herd who received his marching orders as a result, followed quickly by Mulhall. Sunderland fans invaded the pitch and play was held up for four minutes. At the final whistle there was further trouble with Willie Bell punched by a Sunderland thug and Les hit on the head by a glass bottle. Elsewhere, earlier in the season in the League Cup fourth round, away at West Ham United, Leeds inexplicably lost 7-0.

Oddly enough, if Leeds and Sunderland had drawn the FA Cup match again, it would have been replayed two days later, on 2 March. Leeds were already scheduled to play on that date, away at Bologna in the Inter-Cities Fairs Cup, so they would have been forced to field two separate first teams to complete the two ties.

1967 TO 1970 – LEEDS' TIME AND TURN FOR GLORY?

After narrowly beating Manchester City in the sixth round, Leeds' FA Cup challenge would be terminated at the semi-final stage at Villa Park in the most contentious of circumstances. Chelsea, the better team in the first half, led 1-0 at the interval. Leeds improved considerably in the second and were pressing hard for the leveller. They thought they had it late on, in the 83rd minute, when a Terry Cooper strike beat goalkeeper Peter Bonetti low to his left, but Cooper was almost immediately flagged for offside by the linesman and the goal disallowed by referee Ken Burns. In the closing seconds of the 90 minutes, though, came the controversy which has barely subsided since.

There were reports that the London gangland criminals Reggie and Ronnie Kray attended the match, and were photographed with the referee beforehand. Sceptics would simply dismiss the claim as sour grapes on Leeds' part and that no such photo ever existed in the first place as the meeting never occurred. Also, the Kray twins were not known to be football fans. To counter this: they were keen on gambling, and it is entirely plausible that they would resort to bribing a referee (or blackmailing him with threats of violence) if it meant they could make a financial killing on match bets. Regardless of whether or not one entertains such a theory, there was something undeniably malodorous about referee Burns disallowing Peter Lorimer's astonishing strike, with Burns claiming to have not blown his whistle to signal to John Giles to take the initial free kick.

A positive consequence of the previous season's World Cup win was that certain England men were looked upon more favourably by the press than they probably had been before. For Leeds, those men were Jack Charlton, Norman Hunter and Les, of course. Jack would be named the Football Writers' Association Player of the Year for 1967, despite missing a third of the league season injured. Ramsey, knighted in 1967 to become Sir Alf Ramsey, continued his uneasy relationship with the media, so it is a possibility that reporters looked to other men in the camp who were more receptive to interviews and the like. Les preferred to keep out of the limelight when he could but he was a popular chap; sometimes he had no choice in the matter anyway, plus he was more approachable than he let on. In September 1966, he featured in a witty piece in the *Daily Mirror*, which reported, 'Not to be taken seriously quote from Leeds United trainer [and keen golfer] Les Cocker after golf balls had been thrown at goalkeeper Gary Sprake during last weekend's match at Burnley – "I was disgusted. There wasn't one decent ball among 'em!"'

Les's near addiction to golf was shared by son Dave, who continues to be a very good player to this day. They would fit in a round whenever possible, once Les's work was done for the day. This would often include Sundays, after Les had helped at Elland Road with the treatment of knocks and injuries from Saturday's matches. And while Albert Johanneson was at the club, Les's duties (and Dave's) extended to driving to Albert's home to transport him to Elland Road as it was, apparently, deemed unsafe for him to travel on public transport in those times. Finally, when the time came, the Cockers would play a round of golf against the Revies – Don and son Duncan – either at Sandmoor or Temple Newsam. Dave informed me that his and his dad's real 'derby' or grudge match was always against Billy Bremner and Billy Bremner junior.

In the close season of 1966/67, England's under-23s completed a three-match tour in May and June. Spurs boss Bill Nicholson was now in charge and so another new man for Les to work to, as trainer and with Dr Phillips as medical officer. The three got on very well together, as friends and professionals sharing mutual respect. Leeds players Paul Reaney and Jimmy Greenhoff were in the squad. The England group would leave London on 29 May and play Greece in Athens two days later, Bulgaria in Sofia on 4 June and Turkey in Ankara another three days on.

The first two internationals on the tour were drawn: 0-0 with Greece and 1-1 against Bulgaria. The match against Bulgaria was very physical and not without incident. Cyril Knowles was injured following a vicious Bulgarian tackle. Les sprinted on to the field to attend to the injury and almost immediately called on Dr Phillips to assist him. On the field, as Phillips examined Knowles, a group of Bulgarian first-aid personnel tried to intervene by dragging the player on to their stretcher. Les was enraged and gesticulated to them to leave him alone, and spectators angrily threw stones, cans and bottles at the England men. Knowles eventually got to his feet and the game was able to continue but projectiles continued to be thrown at Phillips and Les as they walked around the pitch back to the dug-out. Back in England the following day, headlines read 'England Doctor Stoned in Bulgaria!'

The game against Turkey didn't really improve for Les and Dr Phillips. Match reports told of the Turkish crowd hurling bottles on to the pitch and stones at them while they were treating England's Ralph Coates on the touchline. At the end though, while white-helmeted riot police broke up scuffles on the terraces, the England players were cheered from the stadium. The 3-0 win apparently delighted a 200-strong contingent of British filmmakers who were there on location for the movie *The Charge of the Light Brigade*.

1967/68

This was the season when Leeds proved to the critics that they were nothing like 'chokers' or perennial bridesmaids. Revie had spent big on bringing in England under-23 centre-forward Mick Jones from Sheffield United for £99,999. It would prove to be money well spent. In the First Division, however, Leeds came fourth, on 53 points, with only one defeat at home but ten on the road, five points behind winners Manchester City. In the FA Cup, a careless mistake from Gary Sprake led to a penalty for Everton, which they scored, winning the semi-final 1-0.

The 1968 League Cup

As was usual, the first trophy in English football to be settled each season was the Football League Cup, and the 1967/68 final took place on 2 March 1968 at Wembley. There were two doubts for the Leeds team, John Giles and Jimmy Greenhoff. With Les, both flew down to Weybridge where United's hotel base for the final was, on the Friday night, and would each have a fitness test on the morning of the match. Giles had had flu and Greenhoff had been toiling with a swollen knee; both were passed fit.

Leeds had quite comfortably eased their way to the final, beating Luton Town, Bury, Sunderland, Stoke City and, over two legs in the semi-final, Derby County. They would meet Arsenal at Wembley. It was a tense and tough affair, and would be regarded as one of the most notorious finals played in English football. Having said that, the one goal scored was something of a screamer. It had come in the 18th minute when Eddie Gray aimed a customary corner kick at Jack Charlton standing close to the goal line in between the goalposts, but the ball marginally eluded Charlton and was headed clear to Terry Cooper who instantly whacked a fabulous volley high in to the net from the edge of the box. Having opened that precious advantage, Leeds were not going to let it slip, concentrating on defence for the duration. At the final whistle their players could hardly contain their delight; they had won the first major trophy in the club's history. And they hadn't finished just yet.

The 1968 Inter-Cities Fairs Cup

The route to this season's Inter-Cities Fairs Cup Final would take Leeds, in the away legs of each round, to Luxembourg, Yugoslavia, three times to Scotland and, finally, Hungary. The teams disposed of were, respectively, Spora Luxembourg (16-0 on aggregate), Partizan Belgrade (3-2), Hibernian (2-1), Rangers (2-0), Dundee (2-1) and, in the competition's final, Ferencváros, 1-0 over the two matches. The first leg had been at Elland Road in August, with Mick Jones scoring the solitary goal; the match in Hungary, a month later, stayed goalless, thanks in large part to a sublime display by Gary Sprake in goal. Leeds were the new – and first British – winners of the Inter-Cities Fairs Cup.

* * *

Images of Les carrying injured Leeds players off the football pitch were becoming quite common by now. Whether or not the player was heavier and taller than he, it mattered not, Les had little difficulty carrying that extra luggage. Normally it would be by way of the 'fireman's lift' method (Les 'flopping' the player over his shoulder); occasionally like a guitarist bearing a particularly big guitar. The latest incidence of this was against Rangers at Ibrox on 26 March 1968, with Jimmy Greenhoff suffering a bad injury to his ankle. Les first had to carry Greenhoff off the pitch to the touchline to try and attend to the injured ankle, and then carry him further to the dressing room as the match was over for the blond-haired casualty.

1967 TO 1970 – LEEDS' TIME AND TURN FOR GLORY?

A couple of years ago I was scolded by a highly placed Leeds city official, a lady, for describing football in the 1960s and 70s as a 'real man's game'. Fair enough, it was a poor choice of words on my part. The real point I was trying to make was that professional football in those days was tougher, and that 'crunching tackles', 'bruising challenges' and '50-50 balls', as well as 'ambulance passes', were commonplace and allowed by the referees, and therefore more impact injuries to players occurred. Matches are much more 'civilised' these days, and certainly football pitches are superior in comparison, but whether the drama and excitement is as good, well that's for the individual to decide. I must say though, regardless of whether standards of match officiating have improved or not, I would actually applaud a referee for red-carding a player for blatantly telling him to fuck off. Still, there would probably be too few players left on the pitch to complete the match.

John Giles missed nearly half of that 1967/68 season with a back injury. He would learn from specialists that the problem stemmed from his childhood when he used to jump off walls and suchlike, and had gradually 'flattened' his hip bones. It took quite some time before a recommended treatment resolved the issue. The advice to Giles was to take mud and peat baths on Mondays, Wednesdays and Fridays, and brine baths on Tuesdays and Thursdays, for a total of ten weeks. Harrogate in North Yorkshire had a spa which could serve his recuperative needs perfectly and, lo and behold, the treatment worked.

I was interested to know, were injuries ever down to the Leeds squad being overtrained or playing too many games, and could the club have provided better treatment? Giles said, 'When you're injured, it's not an easy time. You're down and you can feel isolated, not consciously, not by design, but Les was very good. The players would normally go home after training but if you were injured then you'd stay at the ground and get your medical treatment and any training in the afternoon. Les was brilliant at that. A few of the lads would stay on after training to do a bit of practice if you felt you needed it. Well, you always need to improve, there's always something, but you had to be careful to not overdo any of it before a matchday, because we were nearly always playing two matches per week all through the season, and when it got really busy we often played three times in a week. There were 42 league matches per season then, plus the cup competitions. Les wouldn't let us train too much.

'The main important part of football training is done in pre-season. You have to work really, really hard in pre-season and that then sets you up for the season itself, unless you get injured of course and then you have to go through it all again. Once the season was under way, Les's training was all set up to make sure you were at your best fitness for the next match. In our first season in the First Division, 1964/65, we had a lot of matches as you know, as we finished runners-up in the league championship and in the FA Cup. The next season, because we qualified for Europe, the training had to be reassessed but players have also got to look after themselves. It's no good having all the training if a player isn't prepared to look after himself after training has finished. I think when Don first came to Leeds there might have been a few players who weren't as professional as they should have been, and so, when he became manager, he got rid of a few because they didn't look after themselves properly.'

Dave Cocker mentioned to me that the Leeds players, on their return to Elland Road from the end-of-season break, would be 'bricking it' in fear of having put weight on. Any players guilty of weight gain were castigated by Les and Revie, and then had to train harder in hope of losing the excess pounds. The weigh-ins were often done in the changing room in front of all the other players, so plenty of ribbing went on. Giles said he didn't remember any major culprits in all his time there.

Back to the subject of injuries, I asked him if a long-term injury could be damaging to a player's mental health. 'You're not with the lads. I had a long-term injury that wasn't diagnosed for some time, so I was with Les for long spells of time and he was great at keeping the morale up. I had a problem with my back early on, and I tried playing but it was getting worse and I was getting fed up with it, y'know? It was eventually diagnosed and cured but my morale was way down and so I was in with Les in the treatment room a lot. He helped me get right as rain. The fit lads came in to work and went out for training as usual but when you're injured, you're in the medical room all the time and it's not a nice situation. You need someone to get you going and to do the training every day in the right way and the right manner. That's what Les did, and the bond is very close at times like that, as it's very easy to get down when you're injured and it can be a horrible experience when you're doing all the hard work without the enjoyment of playing with the football. You work hard, very hard, at your training but generally speaking you don't see the ball.'

In May 1968, after beating Spain 2-1 in Madrid in the second leg of the European Championship quarter-final, the England party returned. Demonstrating how little respect the 'suits' of the Football Association held for Sir Alf Ramsey, in his autobiography Dr Neil Phillips recalled, 'On returning back from Spain, Alf, Harold, Les and I made our way back to FA headquarters at Lancaster Gate. We were busily returning the team's kit to an area in the basement, when Denis Follows, the FA secretary, joined us. I then witnessed the animosity that existed between Alf and Denis Follows. Pointing to a load of blue boxes embossed with FA shields and stacked on shelves, Alf asked what they were. Denis Follows informed us that each box contained eight table and drinks mats depicting the football grounds where all the 1966 World Cup matches had been held here. Alf asked to see them so Denis opened one box. Inside were eight beautifully coloured aerial photos of the grounds. The photos were hermetically sealed and of very high quality.

'Alf said to Denis Follows, "I'd like to give a set of these mats to each of my staff."

"'I'm sorry, you and your staff can't have any. They have been produced for FA Council members and overseas dignitaries. You and your staff do not qualify."

'Alf exploded, "That's ridiculous. The players and my staff won the World Cup, not the FA Council members. We've now qualified for the finals of the European Championship. Are you really telling me we can't have a set of table mats? I want each of my staff to have a set."

"'I'm sorry but that is not possible."'

1968/69

A fantastic season for Revie's Leeds, winning the First Division title for the first time in their history. Leeds finished with six points more than second-placed Liverpool, and set a few new records on the way. With two points for a win and one for a draw, their total points of 67 from a maximum of 84 was the highest ever, and Leeds won the most home games (18) and earned the most home points (39); their 27 league wins in a season was the highest also, and the total of two defeats the fewest. And the league goals conceded, 26, the lowest. More good news came with Revie being named Manager of the Year.

Leeds' chances of the FA Cup disappeared at the first stage, albeit after a replay, while the team went out of the League Cup earlier than anticipated too, in the fourth round. As for Europe, having knocked out Belgian league leaders Standard Liège, and then Italian side Napoli by way of the good fortune of winning the coin toss with the aggregate scoreline at 2-2, West German side Hannover 96 were then easily disposed of. However, Újpesti Dózsa of Hungary came next, winning 1-0 at Elland Road and 2-0 in Budapest against an illness-ravaged Leeds side.

Anyone in Leeds visiting a newsagent or newspaper shop on Saturday, 1 February 1969 might have noticed a *Yorkshire Post* advertisement placard nearby. On it were the words, in nice big capitals, legible from across the road no doubt, 'LES COCKER FINED'. This whole situation came about at Hillsborough on 4 January, with Sheffield Wednesday playing Leeds in the FA Cup third round. The FA Cup was always a big event – the competition mattered so much more to everyone then – and matches were often tight affairs, this one certainly no exception. Plus, Leeds had never won it. This tie was keenly contested, usually the case between the two Yorkshire teams. In the Leeds dugout, with Revie and substitute Rod Belfitt, Les was desperately keen for the team to win but had been unimpressed with the efforts of Peter Lorimer. Standards were always high at Leeds and Les had become increasingly annoyed at Lorimer's apparent lack of effort. Finally, Les could contain himself no longer, shouting some 'colourful' criticisms at the player. Unfortunately for him, a police officer in the vicinity of the dugout heard every word of the barrage, and he was not a happy bobby. Consequently, the officer formally cautioned Les and, within days of the match, a summons had arrived in Leeds for him, ordering him to attend court in Sheffield to answer a charge of using foul and abusive language in public. The case went ahead, and while the court transcripts are not available, it's easy to imagine that the proceedings went similarly to this:

Judge: 'Mr Cocker, did you call the Leeds United player, Peter Lorimer, a fucking lazy bastard?'

Les: 'Yes I did, your honour.'

Judge: 'And why was that?'

Les: 'Because he was being a fucking lazy bastard, your honour.'

Judge: 'Fined ten pounds!'

At the end of the 1968/69 season, England had a short South American tour scheduled. Dr Neil Phillips outlined some of the preparatory work needed, including blood tests on the players, on 5 May, which was 'the first time the players as a group had undergone any such tests'. Typical of the players, they decided to hold a sweepstake on the results: everyone put in £1, the one with the highest blood level would scoop the pool, the player with the lowest would get his money back. The results were announced, Norman Hunter hit the jackpot and Brian Labone got his money back. Typically, too, Jack Charlton objected to the result as he claimed all the Leeds players had an unfair advantage in that they had been taking iron tablets for weeks, under Dr Adams who, incidentally, Dr Phillips had high regard for.

In June on that tour, England played against Mexico, Uruguay and Brazil. They drew 0-0 in Mexico City, beat

Uruguay 2-1 in Montevideo and lost to Brazil in Rio, 2-1. Dr Phillips wrote that, while in Montevideo, Terry Cooper developed a very nasty bout of tonsillitis, with enlarged glands in his neck. He responded to antibiotics but was unable to play in the Uruguay or Brazil games. Cooper told Dr Phillips that he not infrequently suffered with tonsillitis so, at the end of the tour and back in Britain, the doctor wrote to Leeds suggesting Cooper be referred to an ear, nose and throat specialist. The club followed the advice, Cooper was referred and soon after had his tonsils removed. For the Brazil match at the Maracanã Stadium, Dr Phillips told of the heat already being close to unbearable but, when the England team entered their dressing room to prepare for the match, the door was locked and it also seemed that the central heating was on high, for around 90 minutes. The England party, disgusted and very angry, went on to lose 2-1, conceding two late goals. The players were said to be 'devastated' – it was more than just a friendly for them.

1969/70

The season started well for the new champions, Leeds winning the Charity Shield by beating Manchester City 2-1 at Elland Road on 2 August and watched by nearly 40,000. Eddie Gray and Jack Charlton scored the goals in Allan Clarke's debut match. Fixture congestion would hurt Leeds' hunt for silverware, playing three games in four days from 1 to 4 April 1970. In total they would play 63 matches – 42 in the First Division, 20 in cups and the one Charity Shield tie – and the European Cup would take them to Norway, Hungary, Belgium and Scotland.

The Belgian opponents were the country's champions, Standard Liège, on 4 March 1970. Torrential rain had put the match in doubt, the pitch practically waterlogged, so Liège had enlisted the use of a helicopter to hover above it in efforts to blow the water away. It certainly helped, and the match went ahead, with Leeds winning 1-0. Beforehand, the Leeds team and staff had received a distinctly cold welcome too, with two Liège officials guarding the gates to the stadium and refusing entry to the team's bus, allegedly not recognising that it was the official coach with the players onboard. As well as this, the two gatemen apparently were refusing to talk or explain their stubbornness, and so the coach simply stood there for ten or so minutes, waiting for the men to do something. Revie eventually asked Les and Dr Adams to try and resolve the matter. The pair got off the coach to ask the men what the problem was, but received no response or cooperation. This was, of course, unacceptable, and so Les made a move to open the gates himself. A scuffle ensued, culminating with the two Leeds men – both ex-forces by the way, Les of the army and Adams a paratrooper – flooring the stubborn Liège sentries. At least the Standard Liège players were more respectful to Leeds after the match, praising their performance in their victory.

Elland Road and Hampden Park hosted the two European Cup semi-final legs, 'the Battle of Britain', between Leeds and Celtic. Celtic elected to use Hampden rather than their own ground Celtic Park, as demand for tickets was so high. The numbers proved it had been a sound choice – the Hampden attendance of 136,505 remains UEFA's highest, though there are claims that there were even more, thousands more, there.

Allan Clarke

Allan joined Leeds on 24 June 1969 from Leicester City. His professional career began in 1963 for Walsall, and he signed for Fulham in 1966. 'When he arrived at Fulham, we got on well straight away. I looked after him for a while and my wife Daphne got on very well with Allan's wife Margaret,' said George Cohen, who was not surprised to see Clarke move on to 'bigger things' from Fulham to Leicester for the then British record fee of £150,000. He stayed at Filbert Street for just one full season, however, as Revie came in for him, setting a new domestic transfer record of £165,000.

John Giles wrote about Clarke's first days at Elland Road, on the Fullerton Park training pitches, 'When he came to Leeds he was with Les Cocker on the touchline watching the rest of us training – "That's Billy Bremner, he's a star ... That's Peter Lorimer, he's a star ... That's Eddie Gray, he's a star..." Les went through the whole squad, describing us all as stars, to emphasise to Allan that he was now just a star among many.'

On the subject of transfers, Leeds were relatively wealthy thanks to the remarkable rise under Revie and the generosity of Harry Reynolds, that fine chairman and club custodian. But the transfer budget was by no means limitless, parts of the stadium needed expanding and renovating, for one thing. The United scouting system continued to be invaluable for the 'conveyor belt' of youth players at Elland Road; chief scout Maurice Lindley had been promoted to assistant manager in 1965 but, as always, the entire backroom staff continued with the talent-spotting. Particularly helpful in that regard was Les, thanks to his England work creating more opportunity to see young players of high quality in action. If a player caught his attention, he compiled reports and relayed the information back to Revie. Revie would then decide whether or not to pursue the matter. If the decision was a yes then he, along with Lindley or Les or perhaps all three, would investigate further. This could include European travel. Even if Les's search came to nothing – as in the case of Johan Cruyff, by the mid-1960s already considered as very hot property – it helped his report-writing, and the infamous 'dossiers'. The dossiers were not so dissimilar to the process of businesses conducting SWOT profiles to analyse strengths, weaknesses, opportunities and threats in business plans, though it is easy to understand why certain Leeds and England players would tire of dossier lessons and homework.

Clarke, Leeds' most expensive signing of the 1960s, with that delightful and distinctive Black Country accent which makes a 'cup of tea' sound like a kipper tie, told me of his early dealings with Les, 'He saw me in the flesh before the Gaffer [Revie] did. He was with Alf Ramsey's England and was trainer of the England under-23s. When I made my debut for the England under-23s I think I was a late replacement for Peter Osgood who'd broken his leg. I was playing for Fulham at the time. I actually made my debut going back home as it was Molineux where I'd watched lots of Wolverhampton games back in the 1950s.

'Funnily enough, the night before the England match, Alf took us to Selhurst Park to watch Crystal Palace against my first club Walsall, in the Third Division. The next night [12 October 1966] at Molineux was England against Wales under-23s and we stuffed them 8-0 and I got four of the goals. Not a bad debut! I think Les saw then, and realised for the first time, that I'd be a great Leeds United player. I often asked him if that was the case and he said, "Not half, from that night I wanted you at Leeds," but it took a few years before it actually happened.'

Did Clarke know much about Les before then? 'As a player, Les wasn't a big lad by any means but he was a striker and was "fiery", he had a streak about him, a bit like myself. He was only little like but he could look after himself – if you kick me, pal, I'll kick you back, twice as hard. My striking partner, Mick Jones, never did that though. If anyone kicked Mick I'd kick them back on his behalf. If Mick Jones ever kicked anyone then it will have been an accident! Les was a lovely, lovely man and we all loved him dearly, the Gaffer and all the players and all the staff. On a Monday morning we'd train and have circuits in the gymnasium at Elland Road as well. The Gaffer would make us run round Elland Road and then have Les, as the trainer, in the gym making us work really hard. Billy

Bremner and I used to nickname him Hitler because we were suffering, and he'd just laugh at us. But what a lovely, lovely, loyal and honest man he was, I loved him to bits.'

Did Clarke think Les had any enemies in the game? 'No, no – I mean, I've got a lot of friends from other clubs, and people like Mike Summerbee, Denis Law, even with Liverpool and Bill Shankly and the staff there, always spoke very highly of Les Cocker, they really did. And all the England lads I played with, like Bobby Moore, Bobby Charlton, Alan Ball, Martin Peters, all of them, all had the greatest respect for him. Every single one of them. But with Les being a part of that era, that group, that team, that squad, unless you were a Leeds fan then everybody, the rest of the country, absolutely hated Leeds United because we stuffed everybody! That's the only reason I can come up with, if he had any critics or enemies, that's all it was, maybe jealousy as we were the top team. The Leeds fans knew that, and that's why I love them to this day. If any team wanted to win something, they had to get by us to achieve it. We were one of the greatest teams this country has ever seen and is ever likely to see.'

Did Clarke think Revie would have succeeded without Les? 'I played for two of the greatest managers there ever was: the Gaffer and Alf Ramsey. When I talk about "the Gaffer", everyone knows who I'm talking about, and that's the respect I had for him. In Les and Syd Owen, Bob English, Maurice Lindley, Cyril Partridge, he had an absolutely loyal backroom staff, and you need that as a manager. What I'm saying is that the Gaffer would trust his life with Les Cocker, and Syd and Bob and that, you know what I mean?

'If you were injured as a player, you wouldn't be able to train with the rest of the lads, you'd be getting treatment. I can remember, if I was ever injured, I'd have three or four lots of treatment each day. Our club doctor, Doc Adams, would come down to Elland Road at half past nine in the morning after his general practice surgery nearby in Beeston, and he'd have a chat with our physio Bob English and if anyone was injured the doc would tell him what sort of treatment to give them. So if we couldn't go out and train, we'd be getting treatment and then go in the back room and go on this exercise bike and what have you, and do body work as well, because that's all you could do, until the doctor said you could go out and train as normal with the rest of the lads.

'If I was injured I used to go back to Elland Road for more treatment at six o'clock and if Bob English couldn't do it then Les would be in at six to give me the treatment that the doctor had said I needed. And I remember, going back, my mother-in-law, my Marg's mother, she had a few problems with hard skin on her feet, so I asked Les about arranging a chiropodist with the club to see her. Les told me to bring her down to Elland Road one Monday or Tuesday night and he worked on her feet and resolved the issue himself. She was delighted and wanted to pay him but he wasn't having any of it, he did it because she was my mother-in-law and part of my family and the Leeds family, and that's how good and kind he was. Dedicated, and like the rest of us he absolutely loved that club. It always makes me very happy to know that Les was there with the Gaffer from the start in the Second Division and helped put Leeds United on the world map, and I'm so grateful to Les as he must have kept on at the Gaffer for me to sign.'

* * *

With the World Cup finals held every four years, England would be defending their title as holders in the 1970 tournament in Mexico. Les was involved in most of the preparations for the England party's travel, stay and match arrangements, all a huge task adding to his mountains of work as Leeds participated in probably their busiest phases ever, on and off the pitch. Several Leeds players had patriotic hopes of playing for their country in Mexico too, though sadly England were the only ones to qualify (as defending champions) while the other home nations, and the Republic of Ireland, failed to advance through their respective qualification groups.

The English lads at Elland Road with a realistic chance of playing in Mexico, or at least being named in the 22-man squad, were Paul Reaney, Paul Madeley, Terry Cooper, Norman Hunter, Jack Charlton (even at the age of 35 by the time of the tournament), Mick Jones and Allan Clarke. As it would transpire, Jones would be one of England's 12 reserves, meaning that he would receive all the necessary inoculations and documentation for Mexico but would only need to travel out to join the party if called upon. You will see that the six other Leeds players' World Cup stories all twisted and turned as the 1969/70 season progressed.

To commemorate England's participation in the Mexico World Cup, April 1970 witnessed the release of the England squad's 'Back Home' single. Written by Scotsman Bill Martin and writing partner Phil Coulter – they wrote 'Puppet On A String' for Sandie Shaw and 'Congratulations' for Cliff Richard – the record had session musician Reg Dwight on backing vocals, too. That's the man we know today as Elton John. Dr Neil Phillips stated that he was the only member of England's backroom staff present, though Les was certainly present in the television studio for the single's *Top of the Pops* rendition, standing between Ralph Coates and Terry Cooper, almost certainly miming and definitely looking slightly uncomfortable. Dr Phillips wrote, 'We sang terribly and in addition to the single, we recorded an album too [*The World Beaters Sing the World Beaters*] and they were sung equally as bad. But when the recordings were played back to us, they sounded quite acceptable. It was amazing how the studio gear made us sound so good. It sold so well that Pye gave us all a silver disc.' And Les was one such lucky recipient. Now here's a quiz question for you, folks, a Dave Cocker favourite – in pop history, how many Cockers have earned a silver disc for their record sales? Most people answer 'Two – Jarvis and Joe Cocker' but you now know that the correct answer is three as you can add Les to that pair.

In James Ruppert's splendid *World Cup Cortinas* book, the author tells of England taking their own Leyland coach and drivers with them, rather than having to rely on vehicles and drivers, in foreign climes, they were unacquainted with. Meanwhile, the top players had promotional opportunities too, such as Bobby Moore getting £3,000 from Kellogg's for a Corn Flakes advertisement, and the vinyl record was a sure sign that they wanted to improve on the poor (off-field) showing of 1966 when the victorious players earned relatively little. This time around, they employed an agent to act on their behalf and it was decided to share – including Les and Harold Shepherdson but not Ramsey – all the income. It was decided to endorse certain products and services with a 'Chosen by England' strapline and lion rosette logo. 'Included were BOAC, Esso, Findus and Ford. It's believed that they earned at least £5,000 each from this, plus a Ford Cortina 1600E,' wrote Ruppert. We know though that not every player was given a Cortina – Jack Charlton wanted a Zodiac instead as it was larger and thus big enough for his fishing tackle. It was silver in colour while the Cortinas were all identical in ermine white.

Cruelly, Paul Reaney's World Cup was over before it had even begun. The right-back broke his left tibia bone during a night match at West Ham on 2 April, falling awkwardly after a tackle with the hosts' Keith Miller. Les accompanied Reaney in the ambulance to the London Hospital – the player stayed overnight – and Les visited him, along with Revie and Sprake, the following morning. As well as the Mexico tournament, the injury ruled Reaney out of Leeds' European Cup semi-final second leg at Celtic and the FA Cup Final with Chelsea. As a matter of straightforward protocol, Ramsey was soon informed about the incident; he would have to select a replacement so asked Les if Reaney's team-mate, Paul Madeley, would be a worthy replacement? Madeley was renowned, at least around Elland Road, for his marvellous ability to play in practically every outfield position; he was a virtuoso of versatility. Les informed his England boss how good Madeley was as a full-back. There was never any bias with Les, he genuinely believed Madeley was the perfect solution, and Ramsey trusted his judgement. He instructed Les to tell Madeley that he was now in the England World Cup squad. On receiving the news, Madeley told Les how delighted and honoured he was to be included. Shortly after, however, Madeley got back to Les to give him 'backword', a family holiday had already been booked and he wanted to go on it as he needed a break. Les was quite astonished, though of course he appreciated Madeley's predicament. Everton's Keith Newton replaced Reaney instead.

Due to a reported gastroenteritis endemic in Mexico, Dr Phillips had to impose stringent food and drink regulations on the entire England squad and staff. The conditions over there were far from ideal anyway, and Phillips as well as Ramsey, Les and Shepherdson were under no illusions of how demanding their own work was to be to ensure the good welfare of the England players. No water, other than bottled, was to be drunk, and teeth cleaning should also use only bottled water.

No salads, unpeeled fruit or ice cream to be eaten, and no meals were to be eaten other than those prepared and provided by the England officials. And room service in the hotels must not be used. Everyone was to wash their hands before every meal and, particularly, after the toilet. Phillips arranged for the antibacterial solution, Phisohex, to be supplied to every player to be used for washing purposes.

Former Leeds player Freddie Goodwin, out in North America as he was managing a team in Florida, offered to aid England's cause as he was used to coping with players working in extreme heat. And Mexico 1970 would be extremely hot, not least because the matches were scheduled for midday each time, a ludicrous – and potentially dangerous – decision just for the sake of international television. Goodwin suggested a glucose saline drink called Gatorade, and the company who produced it made available supplies to the England base in Mexico. A slight snag materialised when the Mexican authorities objected as there was no license for Gatorade drinks to be used there. Gatorade resolved this by specially producing it in powder form, and Phillips completed the process by using Malvern bottled water to dissolve the powder in. To help the players acclimatise better to the extreme heat, England would have newly designed kits too – the shirts and shorts would be revamped to all be light in colour so as to reflect the heat away, with dark colours known to absorb radiant heat. England's strip was thus registered as all white and all light blue. Not only that, the Umbro shirts were made with a quite revolutionary material called Aertex, a 'cellular cotton fabric' which, simply put, provided more ventilation in the garments. The shorts also had Aertex bands at the sides and contained a pocket, as requested by the players.

The English press wrote countless pieces during the run-up to the finals, generally supportive of Ramsey and his men, while in his autobiography, an excellent book, Dr Phillips published a personal diary of events years later. On 4 May, one newspaper reported, 'England's official reunion came yesterday afternoon when the players assembled for tea at a hotel near the FA's Lancaster Gate headquarters. There, trainers Harold Shepherdson, Les Cocker and medical officer Dr Neil Phillips gave them a brief check-up.' Later, a 27-man squad flew to Mexico City, with Francis Lee due to follow a few days later. On their chances of retaining the World Cup, Ramsey told the media, 'I think we have an excellent chance and that we have a stronger party than in 1966.' There would, though, be problems, in various areas involving various England men.

Dr Phillips wrote, 'Day five in Mexico brought our first major casualty. In continuing to unpack the various heavy boxes of equipment, Les Cocker injured his back. Clinically, I formed the opinion he was suffering from a prolapsed disc in his spine. We arranged x-ray at the ABC Hospital and though Les said he had no history of back trouble, the x-ray revealed a major defect in his lower spine. This amazed me, that he hadn't had any back problems before. He would be confined to bed for several days.' Les would need specialist advice once back in Britain.

On 15 May, the rested and recovered Les was asked about England's planning for the tournament. 'Precision passing in midfield will be the deciding factor in the World Cup,' he said. 'Let's use an old-fashioned word and call it "combination". Any man who goes out there in these conditions and tries to play on his own will kill himself. The individual stuff will have to be saved for around the 18-yard line. That's when we want to see a man take on two or three and have a go in the middle, the ball has got to do the work. It means that every pass must hit the man. That's what we're looking for.'

By 18 May, some of the English press were realising that 'their' England team might not be very popular with the 'Latin Americans'. It was reported in a newspaper, 'Any hostility against England has been created by the Mexican press, angry at being unable to penetrate Alf Ramsey's inner thoughts. Apart from this, it has been a wonderfully beneficial fortnight for England, with Les Cocker saying, "The spirit among the boys is absolutely marvellous. They've really knuckled down to it."'

Two days later, England beat Colombia 4-0 in a friendly, played in the Colombian capital, Bogotá. Jack Charlton did not feature, Brian Labone apparently now Ramsey's first-choice centre-half. On 24 May England beat Ecuador 2-0 in Quito, the capital city and more than 9,000 feet above sea level, even higher than Bogotá, so another useful way to acclimatise to the high altitude. Before the match came to be the real drama, however. Dr Phillips was there and wrote, in his autobiography, 'We were booked in the Tequendama Hotel ... I had dinner and then wandered into the foyer where I noticed the two Bobbys [Moore and Charlton] window-shopping inside a small jewellery shop. The three of us sat on a settee in the hotel lounge immediately outside the shop. Within minutes, a very angry and distressed shop assistant confronted us, "Which one of you has taken the emerald and diamond bracelet? It was you, wasn't it?" pointing at Moore. "You have stolen the beautiful bracelet, I must notify the police." We were astonished.' Phillips then explained that he had reported the matter to Ramsey, 'After supper, I attended a meeting with Alf and the two Bobbys. Alf insisted the three of us report exactly what, if anything, happened in the jeweller's shop. We all claimed total innocence.'

On 25 May, the England party flew back to Bogotá and the Tequendama Hotel again. And there, while the England party watched a special screening of the James Stewart film *Shenandoah*, Moore was arrested. Later, as his team-mates left to return to Mexico City, he remained in Bogotá to face the ludicrous charges. Les stayed in Bogotá, as did two FA officials. It would transpire, but not before the scandal had made the world news, that the allegations were false. The motives for the con, 'set-up' or extortion remained unclear, but a conspiracy against the England team wasn't such an outrageous suspicion.

Two days later, the *Birmingham Daily Post* reported, 'While England's indignant World Cup players await the release of captain Bobby Moore after the theft accusations in Bogotá, the full implications of a Latin American hate campaign are being brought home. The world champions were confronted in Mexico this morning with newspaper headlines which proclaimed "England arrive drunk and incomplete". Another newspaper had a three-picture strip of Jeff Astle flaked out at the airport. He was being treated by trainer Les Cocker for air sickness but the newspaper's caption said he was "under the influence of whisky".'

It was reported on 1 June, 'The training has been ruthless. For 90 minutes Les Cocker has had them going all out, every day. If fitness can win anything then England must top the poll.' But the suds of this particular soap opera frothed with what Dr Phillips called a 'bombshell' from Ramsey, informing his three lieutenants that the four London players in the squad – Moore, Martin Peters, Peter Bonetti and Geoff Hurst – had, instead of being paid for promotional work, negotiated with the companies for their wives to be provided with all-expenses-paid stays in Mexico for the tournament. Ramsey's comment that 'they will stay in a different hotel to the players' failed to lighten the mood among Shepherdson, Les and Dr Phillips, who were quite appalled at the news.

Dr Phillips later wrote, 'Eventually, Les Cocker broke the silence, "Well if this is the case, I think the four players should be told they will not be selected. The arrival of just four wives, after we have been away from home for over four weeks, will cause chaos. What will the other players think? It's disgraceful, it could ruin all our plans. It certainly will affect team morale, the presence of four wives will unsettle everyone. They should be told they can't do it, it's unacceptable." Harold Shepherdson was of similar mind to Les. I suggested it should be an all or nothing situation, either ALL the wives came out to Mexico or none of them.'

Their unease with the situation only increased when, at a later staff meeting with Ramsey, the manager dropped a smaller though still significant bombshell again. Dr Phillips wrote, 'Alf informed us that Lady Ramsey would arrive at similar time to the four players' wives as Alf had been involved as starter with the World Cup Motor Rally and part of his agreement with the organisers was that his wife would be invited to the World Cup tournament.' The four wives now became the five wives. They arrived in Guadalajara before England's first World Cup game against Romania took place, and would be staying in the Camino Real Hotel, Mexico City. Dr Phillips described developments, 'Bizarre stories, real or imaginary, were wickedly spread daily by the 18 players whose wives were still in England. Stories of late-night parties, nude bathing and fanciful behaviour with other residents of the Camino Real Hotel were rapidly invented by many of the England players. There was no truth to these stories but the effect they had on the four players varied enormously ... As far as I was concerned, the presence of the wives was a disaster.'

Notwithstanding, England beat Romania 1-0 with a clever left-footed strike from Hurst, eluding his marker after Alan Ball's cross into the area had deflected to him. Their second match would be in six days' time on 7 June, against Brazil. It would, indisputably, be a tough tie, perhaps the toughest possible, against such a great side, and there certainly was no call for 'locals' to try and increase the pressure on England the night before. But they did. 'The noise commenced as soon as we finished supper at around 8pm,' wrote Dr Phillips. 'It transpired that hundreds of cars had encircled the roads around the Hilton Hotel. Many of them had people sitting on the car bonnets, they banged on drums and tin lids, the car horns hooted, trumpets were blown, the crowd chanted "Brazil". The noise was deafening, Mexican and Brazilian fans burned flags. The police refused to take action.'

Brazil beat England 1-0. Gordon Banks's amazing save against Pelé in the first half helped to place this match in football legend, and England gave the eventual world champions their hardest match of the tournament. It had been a magnificent battle but England finally succumbed to a superb shot by Jairzinho in the second half, after a casual yet perfect lay-off from Pelé had let him in. England's final group match would be against Czechoslovakia, and they needed to at least draw to go through to the quarter-final.

They did more than that, winning 1-0. Hurst was rested and replaced by Allan Clarke, who told me a little about it, 'I made my under-23s debut in 1967 I think it was, but Alf always picked me in the full England squads as well but I never got a game. So, in 1970, we're going to defend the World Cup in Mexico and we were set to be out there for six, six and a half weeks, which is a long time to be without your family, especially if you have young children like I did with my daughter being born in 1968. My wife, Marg, wrote to me while I was out there and used to joke with me that our daughter hadn't forgotten me, yet. I said to Marg, "If I don't get a game, after being with the World Cup winners for around three years, then I won't go again if he picks me in the squad."

'Anyway, we needed to win against Czechoslovakia to qualify for the quarter-finals. The day before the game, Alf Ramsey comes up to me on the training pitch and tells me I'm playing against the Czechs. I said, "That's great boss, thanks," and Alf says, "I think you're ready now," and I replied, "Alf, I've been ready for three years." The same day, in a team meeting, Alf asked us all: if we got a penalty in the match, who would take it? Well I would have put my hand up straightaway but there were all these experienced internationals there so I didn't bother as I thought one of them would do it, bearing in mind this was my debut anyway. But no one was putting their hand up, so I said, "I'll take it, Alf." Alf said, "Good lad," and that was it. Anyway, the match came and, as you know, we won 1-0 and I scored from the penalty spot, sent the goalkeeper the wrong way. After the match, in the England dressing room, Les Cocker said, "Allan, Alf was funny. You know, for the penalty when you were placing the ball on the penalty spot, in the dugout Alf was asking, "Les, will Allan score?" "Pardon, Alf?" "Will Allan score?" "Alf, you can put your mortgage on it," and I put it away, sent the goalie the wrong way.'

Next came West Germany, ruining it all for England who had been 2-0 up through goals from Alan Mullery and Martin Peters. The Germans won 3-2, after extra time, and Ramsey, along with Peter Bonetti in goal, would be blamed for the defeat.

While Les was in Mexico for the World Cup, Dave Cocker borrowed his England Cortina, 'When I dropped Dad off at Whites Hotel, Lancaster Gate, to fly off to Mexico, I had my younger brother with me. We then drove to see 10 Downing Street and I managed to park right outside the famous front door. The copper on duty laughed and had a good look at the badges on the car, he knew exactly what it was! On a drive down to London it was difficult to do it on a tank of petrol, that 1600E really lapped up petrol. It was a good job that Esso provided free fuel. Not only that, the cars were registered to Brentwood police station which meant that if you got a speeding ticket etc it went straight there and you wouldn't hear any more about it.'

Once Les had returned home to Leeds, he paid heed to Dr Phillips's advice and went to hospital for treatment on his back, a spinal operation, no less. This was a risky procedure for which Leeds United brought in a specialist to conduct the operation, at the Leeds General Infirmary. The operation proved successful and it wouldn't be too long before Les was back to full strength.

Les Cocker, inside-forward for Stockport County.

Les in action for Accrington Stanley.

Les Cocker in action for Accrington Stanley v Carlisle United, 1950s.

Les Cocker and Syd Owen leaving Fullerton Park training ground after putting the Leeds players through their paces.

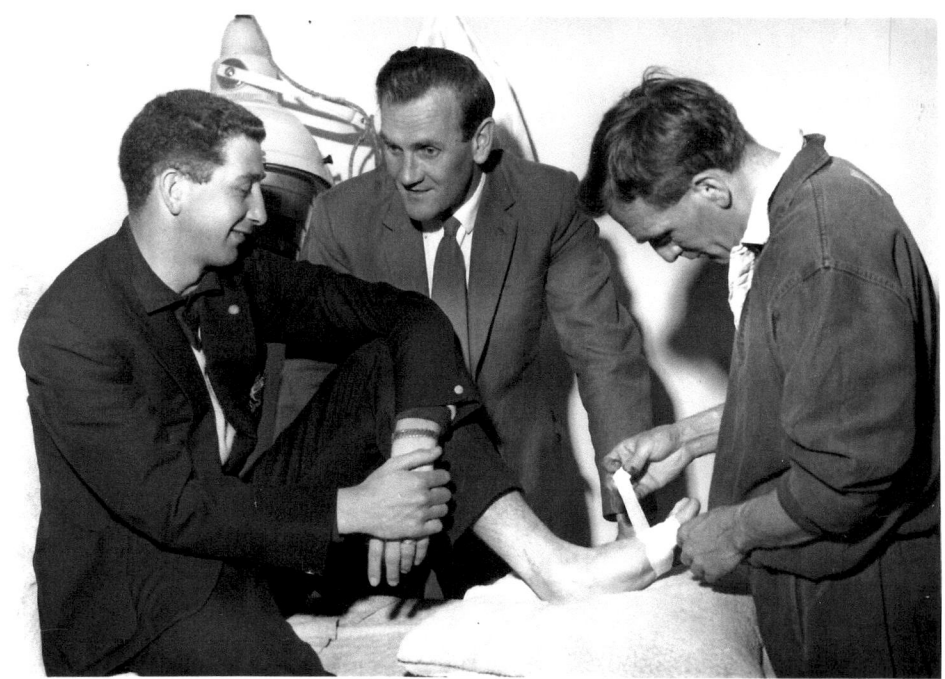

Les in the treatment room administering a bandage to Leeds player Freddie Goodwin in conversation with manager Don Revie.

Leeds United, the original Reservoir Dogs cast? Bobby Collins and Les are top left, the Leeds party on European soil in 1966/67.

Les golfing with friends and England colleagues Harold Shepherdson and Alf Ramsey.

Les pointing the way forward from the Leeds dugout.

A jubilant thumb-up from Don Revie in 1969 after Leeds have secured the league title at Anfield, drawing 0-0 with Liverpool.

Les and his famous globe-trotting teapot!

Les carrying injured Allan Clarke off the pitch during the 1970/71 season.

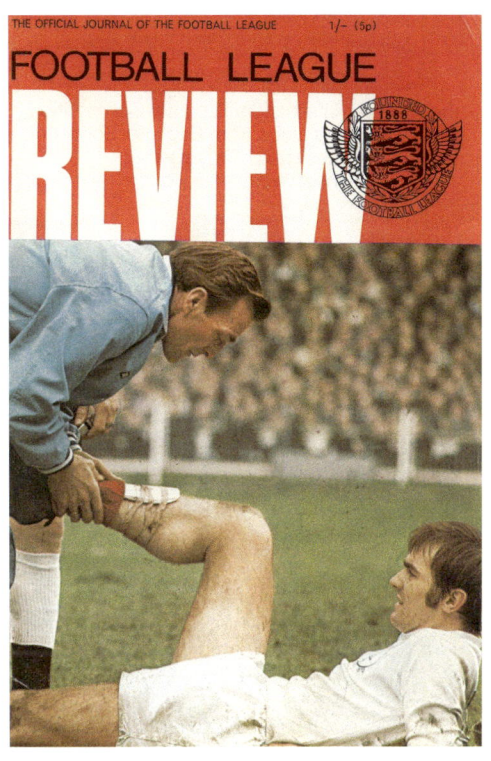

A 1971 issue of the Football League Review, the front cover showing Les giving treatment to Terry Cooper.

Les Cocker scrutinising the Wembley pitch ahead of the centenary FA Cup Final of 1972, the turf in far superior condition to Leeds' previous visit there in 1970!

Les leading the Leeds training in February 1973.

Les Cocker and Don Revie in the dugout, season 1973/74.

Allan Clarke and Dave Cocker with the league championship trophy in 1974.

Les in Czechoslovakia with England in 1975.

The photo is of the England party in Brazil, June 1977, the message written by Don Revie, congratulating Les on managing the team and holding the Brazilians to a 0-0 draw on England's first ever unbeaten tour of South America.

Les Cocker, the new assistant to new England manager Don Revie, outside the FA's Lancaster Gate, July 1974.

7

1970 – Mexico and after

BLACK BOOTS seem to be a real rarity in professional football these days. I've nothing against that, the vast spectrum now available to players is eye-catching, and wearing coloured boots doesn't do any harm to anyone, after all. In a strange way, I see it similar to when coloured vinyl records began to proliferate the charts in the late 1970s – there were cynical rumours that the sound quality on coloured vinyl discs was inferior to black vinyl. My thoughts on that possibility were straightforward – the colour and sound quality of the record mattered not, if it was a shit song it would always be a shit song! So, if a rubbish footballer wore coloured boots instead of black, he'd still be a rubbish footballer. Not that I knew anything about rubbish footballers, of course. What the hell am I rambling on about such nonsense for, I hear you ask?

After leaving school at 15 years of age, painting and decorating had been Les Cocker's original trade. Go forward about 30 years and his handiwork with the paintbrush was to come in handy at his football club. The 1970/71 season witnessed the advent of non-black boots, supplied by the Danish sportswear company Hummel International. Everton's Alan Ball was the player credited as the first to wear their white football boots, and a few more followed suit, including Leeds and England's Terry Cooper. Cooper, though, soon realised that his Hummel boots were not as comfortable as his preferred Puma ones, and so he asked Les to paint his pair of Pumas white and 'modify' them so as to incorporate the Hummel logo. We know that other Leeds players would go on to request their own boots be painted to look like other makers' – due to personal sponsorship deals and the like – but it isn't clear as to whether Les's artistic skills were called on again.

1970/71

After the trauma of the previous season's setbacks, Leeds needed to bounce back and prove they were still a major force. In the league they set off in a hurry, quickly topping the table, where they stayed for most of the season. Their first defeat came in the eighth game, 3-0 at Stoke City, on 12 September (Leeds wearing all-orange for the first and possibly last time). Seven months later, and two months after a huge FA Cup upset with Colchester beating Leeds 3-2 in the fifth round, Revie's men met West Bromwich Albion at Elland Road in a 'must-win' game.

The match was refereed by Ray Tinkler, and Albion controversially won 2-1. Possibly only one person in the stadium considered Albion's crucial second goal as *not* being offside. Regrettably for Leeds (and their title challenge) that one person was Tinkler. Even the linesman for that pitch-half adjudged offside. As a consequence, some incensed Leeds fans encroached on to the pitch, including Dave Cocker, but the referee escaped unharmed, thankfully.

Leeds ended the season in second place and a single point behind champions Arsenal. They would be punished for the pitch 'invasion', the Football League forcing them to play their first four home games of the next season at neutral grounds. Police officer Eric 'Buffer' Brailsford was on duty pitchside at the West Brom match, and, said Dave, 'It was Buffer who saved me when I got on the pitch to remonstrate with Tinkler. Buffer stopped me and said, "Dave, don't be a fucking idiot!" and I begrudgingly took his advice!' Buffer Brailsford was a regular at Elland Road, popular with club personnel and who was training to be a sports physiotherapist. He would work with United and also become Leeds Rugby League's physio and Yorkshire County Cricket Club's. He was like a protective uncle or even bodyguard to Leeds United players and staff.

The Inter-Cities Fairs Cup was United's saving grace this season. They had reached the final after beating Norway's Sarpsborg, East Germany's Dynamo Dresden, Czech side Sparta Prague, Vitória Setubal of Portugal and, in the semi-final, their favourite rivals Liverpool. Leeds would meet Juventus in the two-legged final. The first leg took place in

Juventus' Stadio Comunale on Friday, 28 May, two days after the original scheduled date, the sides drawing 2-2. Three days of heavy rain caused the Wednesday night match to be abandoned after 53 minutes due to the waterlogged conditions, with the score 1-1.

As well as the weather during Leeds' few days in Turin, a couple of other incidents would conspire to make things unsettled and even stormy. During that first abandoned match, Eddie Gray had landed awkwardly on the turf and dislocated a shoulder, a repeat of the same injury he had suffered two weeks before when playing for Scotland. Les was, of course, called into action to attend to Gray. Dislocated shoulders, undoubtedly major injuries, are at least not career-threatening (to outfield players). Later on, Les would be called upon for very different reasons.

By this time, Jim Lister had been Leeds' official coach driver for a couple of years. The 'coach driver of the crown jewels' was highly popular at Elland Road with the players and staff, particularly Don Revie (who was 'the Boss') and Les. Lister was a trusted confidant and loyal servant, and a very nifty driver too, always within the legal limits, of course. He was on driving duty in Turin that week; in fact, he was a one-man chaperone just about too, for the players' wives who had been invited as guests, this being a big occasion, a European final. Lister told Gary Edwards all about it in Gary's brilliantly illuminating *No Glossing Over It*, 'The Boss had arranged for the wives to move into the players' hotel for the Wednesday night before all departing for England the following day but because of the abandonment, the Boss wanted the wives to go home to allow the players to concentrate on the rearranged final two nights later. The wives, understandably, wanted to stay but the Boss hated distractions before a game ... During the after-match banquet at the players' hotel on the Wednesday night, some of the players tried to persuade the Boss to let the girls stay on. The Boss very rarely showed anger but he was livid and he stormed out of the banquet. What is not widely known is that the Boss actually resigned that night.'

Les, having witnessed in Mexico the potential damage to England's World Cup preparations caused by similar 'distractions', was in complete agreement with Revie. Revie felt his authority had been undermined, especially as he had done so much for the benefit of the players and their families, and such apparent ingratitude pained him. Lister confirmed that Revie had left the hotel and booked himself into another one, alone, 'The players were stunned and Jack, Billy and Les spent two hours trying to locate his hotel. Once they did, thankfully they managed to persuade him to return to the hotel. The wives returned home the following day.'

The match itself was a 2-2 draw, Juventus having led twice. Firstly, a Roberto Bettega goal had separated the sides but Leeds fought back, equalising three minutes after the break thanks to a Paul Madeley strike from 25 yards. Twelve minutes later, Juventus' lead was restored with a Fabio Capello snapshot, only for Mick Bates to pounce on a goalkeeping error and coolly strike the ball into the roof of the net, perhaps uttering 'Grazi' to the keeper at the same time.

In the final's second leg, at Elland Road, a warm, sunny evening, all the scoring occurred in the opening 20 minutes; a clinical fine strike from Clarke had given Leeds the lead, soon to be levelled by a fine finish from Pietro Anastasi. For the rest of the match both teams strove for a winner but Leeds, the stronger side, held out; there were no more goals, 1-1 on the night and 3-3 on aggregate, Leeds winning their second Fairs Cup, this time on the away goals rule.

By the close of the 1970/71 season, nine months' duration, Leeds had played 57 competitive matches. During that time, there were also 11 full England or under-23 matches for Les to attend (unless a club/country fixture clash arose, which it did on occasion, then his priority was Leeds). Well over 60 commitments in fewer than 40 weeks, quite a workload, not forgetting all the driving involved, the coach journeys, the flights and overseas travel and stays. Les, though, was indefatigable, a veritable human dynamo.

Nigel Davey

Local lad Nigel Davey joined Leeds as an apprentice in February 1964. He spent one year playing for the juniors before moving up to reserve-team level where he became a regular. A tough, dependable player, probably best known as a full-back – left or right as he was good with both feet – but he could easily adapt to half-back or even inside-forward. Although he would make just 23 first-team appearances, he was regarded as an important part of Revie's squad and his Leeds career was to span ten years.

Davey is very entertaining to interview and we had a couple of hours' fun – between Covid lockdowns – chatting away in a pub not too far away from his home district of Garforth. I asked him about his time at Elland Road and working with Les.

'There was no messing with Les, I can tell you that much straight off. This was during training, around 1971 season. We were having a practice match on Fullerton Park, 11 v 11. Before the game, Les was telling me to take it easy, "We know you can tackle but it's just a practice match, there's nothing to prove." I wasn't a right good footballer but I could tackle properly, like Norman Hunter, for instance. Anyway, during the match, I tackled someone, I think it might have been Eddie Gray, a right rarity for me to do that, obviously. But I tackled him, hard but fair, and he was up in the air as a result. It wasn't a foul but I got him a good one. Then, from the touchline, I heard Les shouting at me, right annoyed, "What have I told you?" It wound me up, it was a good tackle, and I couldn't stop myself and reacted by telling him to fuck off. I thought he might have another go but it all went quiet and the game carried on as normal, without incident.

'Afterwards, walking from the Fullerton pitches down the steps to the West Stand where all the changing rooms were, Les comes up to me and says, "Just hang on there, Nigel," so I did that while everyone else went inside to get washed and changed. Les then comes back out and he's carrying some boxing gloves – two pairs – and tells me to put them on and he'll see me in the gym. The gym was also inside the West Stand so he takes me there and opens the door for me and tells me to put the gloves on. I'm like mid-20s and he's nearer 50 but that made no difference to Les – he says, "Right, come on," meaning we should have a match, a boxing match. And that's it, next thing we're boxing. Well, Les was boxing, I was just getting hit and hit!

'This went on for a bit and after a few minutes he told me to tell him when I'd had enough. I said, "I've had enough NOW, Les" – I'd had enough before it had even started. He'd knocked fuck out of me. So he says, "Have you anything to say to me?" and I said yes and that I was sorry for saying that to him. I mean, I genuinely was sorry, I shouldn't have done it. He said, right calm and reassuringly, "It's all right, it's all right" and told me to go get changed. Back in our changing room – Les and Don and Syd had their own separate one – all the lads were asking where I'd been and why my eyes were red and my lip swollen. "I've been in the gym with Les and he's just given me a good fucking hiding!"'

I told Davey that I bet he always thought better of answering back since that. 'Course, I wasn't stupid!' he answered. 'I genuinely had nothing but respect for him, though. He was a fit little man. He was brilliant, even after he gave me a bit of a bloody battering. He was a good, good man, he always wanted to help you, to improve you. After a Saturday match, on the following Monday he'd always put his arm round you and chat with you and tell you where you'd gone wrong and how you could do better, especially in how to mark your man better. It wasn't a bollocking, it was good, friendly advice. He was a lovely man.'

* * *

After the end of the 1970/71 season, Les was featured in an *Evening Post* tribute, penned by Mike Casey, possibly providing the most information anyone had read about him, 'Les Cocker rolled up the sleeves of his mud-spattered tracksuit, plunged his hands into a sink full of hot water, and murmured with the satisfaction of a man who had completed a good job, "I enjoyed that." On the other side of the wall, in the players' dressing room, Leeds United's £1.5m first-team squad relaxed after a strenuous two-hour stint under the man whose skill, energy and dedication has earned him the reputation of being one of the best trainers in Europe. At that moment, United's stars looked less happy about life than the 5ft 6in stick of human dynamite called Les Cocker. Their main thought was relief at escaping from the drill sergeant's parade ground, also known as the Fullerton Park training pitch.

'Stockport-born Les has been called Soccer's Peter Pan, a tribute to the way the passage of his 48 years have hardly left their mark. "I didn't know what training was all about until I joined United," says Allan Clarke. "I knew Les from my England under-23 days but I had no idea what United's players went through. I'd heard that they were the fittest team in the country, of course, but I didn't know what they had to contend with! Now I'm part of the Elland Road setup I realise what an asset Les is to the club." Don Revie says, "He has proved one of our best signings. I rely on him to knock the lads into shape."

'The blunt-speaking, pipe-smoking Cocker is a familiar sight on Football League grounds in his neat blue tracksuit. But the man behind the figure so often seen galloping across the pitch to tend to an injured player shuns publicity. "All I can ask is to be allowed to do the job United pay me to do – to ensure players are in peak condition on matchday and to help plan tactics," he says. And he means it. He has no ambitions outside Leeds United. His reward is in seeing players win success on the field. His most frustrating moments come during a match when he is in the trainer's dug-out on the touchline. "When I see the boys forgetting what we've planned during the week I must admit my hackles rise. But it's because I feel for the players who work so damned hard at training sessions then forget in the heat of the moment what they've learnt."

'Cocker is as different from the conventional idea of a trainer as United are from the dispirited outfit which wore those blue and old gold shirts when Revie took over ten years ago. Les Cocker is a trainer with his feet firmly planted in the 70s. He is a fully qualified FA coach and has a wide knowledge of medicine and the treatment of injuries. Has he a recipe for success? "No, unless it's to make every training session different. Variety helps the players to maintain interest." His pet hate? "Players who won't put their backs into work all the time." Football and his family are his life. If he has one regret about his career it is that it takes him away from home too much. "My wife has been a wonderful encouragement to me," he says proudly. "She has played a major role in bringing up the children – David 20, Stephen 17 and Ian 12 – and has never complained about my absences with United and England. Last year, for instance, I was away with the club for three months in three or four-day spells, plus the seven weeks I was in Mexico with the World Cup squad. The funny thing is my wife shows no interest in soccer. One of the few matches she attended was the World Cup Final at Wembley in 1966. When the game went into extra time the tension was too much for her so she walked out and paced up and down the terraces at the back of the stands. There she met Nobby Stiles's father, who was in the same state." Surprisingly for one so immersed in professional football, this dynamic little fellow finds he can go home and leave his work behind – "Once I leave the ground I forget the problems," he says.'

8

1972 – t'FA Cup

LES'S WORK roster for England's full squad and the under-23s was particularly crowded for the 1971/72 season, with over a dozen fixtures including away ties in the European Championship for the seniors and a June 1972 tour for the under-23s. Adding in his Leeds United commitments – and let us not forget his dedication to golf – it's a wonder he ever found time to try and relax. Incoming at Elland Road, though he would hardly be physically present there, was Tony Collins who joined as the club's new chief scout. A former left-winger, he first played professionally in 1947, playing for several clubs in the 1950s before finishing at Rochdale, with whom he played until 1961 but managed up to 1967. Tony was the first black manager in the English Football League.

The previous season, with Arsenal winning the Double of First Division and FA Cup, Don Revie challenged his players to emulate the Gunners' fine achievement. In fact, Leeds had a chance of winning an unusual, nay unique, treble due to the Inter-Cities Fairs Cup being abolished and replaced by the UEFA Cup. The Fairs Cup, known by some (100 per cent not including me) as the Noel Beard Trophy, was to be played off between Leeds and Barcelona at their Camp Nou stadium. The winners of the match would become the permanent owners of the trophy. Barcelona were the first champions, back in 1958, and Leeds were the current holders.

The play-off took place on 22 September 1971. There was a starting debut for Joe Jordan, the young centre-forward who had been brought to Les's attention by former Leeds stalwart Eric Smith, and who signed from Morton in 1970. Jordan scored Leeds' only goal in the 2-1 defeat, a match which seems quite insignificant in their history. Incidentally, before flying to Spain, Leeds' players and staff were given cholera vaccinations due to a tiny outbreak of the disease in Huddersfield.

One week later and Leeds were unceremoniously knocked out of the UEFA Cup by little-known Belgian side Lierse SK, 4-2 on aggregate.

It might seem inappropriate for a book like this, a biography of a great football man, to mention off-field football violence – and I do appreciate that view – but football hooliganism had arrived by the early 1970s and was, sadly, on the increase all the while. An ugly blight on the game but relevant at the same time. Hooliganism had existed in English football since the 1950s, steadily growing in the 60s and still on the rise throughout the 70s. The media perhaps tried to ignore it or chose not to feature it in the hope of it just 'going away', but it was definitely happening.

Most clubs had aggressive and violent elements in their supporter ranks, fervently backing their team while making life for visiting teams and fans as uncomfortable as possible. Some enjoyed causing small-scale havoc on their travels to away games, too. Deservedly or not, Leeds supporters had gained such a reputation, undoubtedly heightened by the 'Tinkler effect' from the previous season, but to consider them as the first or the worst sinners would be off-target. Still, the club was bigger news by 1971, despite certain hooligan factions especially from London areas and the north-west involved in scenes of disorder for years already. I only mention this in view of an incident 'prematurely' reported by the press at a West Ham v Leeds game in October 1971.

Following the 6 October midweek League Cup stalemate at Upton Park, newspaper reports described an alleged incident of violence at the ground, the article headlined 'Cocker clears the fans' above the story, 'Leeds United trainer Les Cocker today denied stories of after-the-match hooliganism at Upton Park last night. Cocker said, "All the press reports about brick-throwing incidents and our dressing room window being smashed are wrong. I broke that window." Cocker explained, "There were some young boys outside the dressing room trying to look in. I reached up to close the window, the catch was a bit tight and when I forced it, it broke." Regarding reports that the Leeds United coach driver had been cut by flying glass and received facial injuries, Mr Cocker said, "The driver, Sid Brown, lifted the boot of the coach to remove a couple of baskets and unfortunately hit his head on the catch. That was all that happened." Unfortunately Brown had to have two stitches inserted in the injury. Mr Cocker put through a phone call to West Ham secretary Eddie Chapman, explaining what happened and offering to pay for the broken window. Said Cocker, "It just shows what can be made out of nothing. Some people want to get their facts right. This gives clubs a bad name.'" As an aside, Leeds went on to lose the replay with West Ham at Elland Road, 1-0 after extra time.

Paul 'The Beaver' Trevillion is renowned for his beautifully illustrated comic art realism in newspapers and publications *Tiger*, *Roy of the Rovers* and *Shoot!*, among others. His artistic endeavours are part of Leeds United folklore. He is the man, for instance, who created the player sock tags and Target footballs, and who decided a Leeds cup final single would help the cause, too. As a child, I was quite obsessed with Marvel and DC Comics, but if I had ever been asked who my favourite artist was, the answer probably would have caused a bit of a surprise, 'The fella who does You Are The Ref in *Shoot!*' I was never good at remembering names. That fella was, of course, Paul Trevillion. I barely bothered to read the questions, I was just looking at the brilliant artwork.

I have been lucky enough to interview Trevillion a few times in recent years, ever since we worked together, sort of, raising funds for the Don Revie Statue erected in 2012. He's another proper Londoner, and his bright, warm voice always reminds me of Charlie Drake. Trevillion is quick-witted and a very lively talker, in that voice of his full of warmth and animation. And he has such a wonderful laugh, it's infectious. He was really keen to help with this book, very fond as he clearly was of Les.

'Bill Nicholson's successful Spurs team in the 60s, when they won the Double, were absolutely the fittest team I had ever seen. I watched them in training and Bill was unbelievably demanding. But when I went to see Don Revie, I got the chance to watch the Leeds players train under Les Cocker. And this was the first time I really saw Les Cocker but I did know of him through Don Howe who had studied for coaching badges with England, just like Les had, and Alf and all the England staff spoke well about Les. Now I was seeing it properly for myself for the first time. I was watching the Leeds players training and I couldn't believe what I was seeing. I could not believe how fit they were – and that was compared with Tottenham!

'I kept watching the Leeds players and when the session ended, I remember saying to Don Revie afterwards, "Don, I can't get over it, I can't believe how fit they are." And Don just smiled and said, "You've got to get them fit, Paul. You know, an amateur practices until he gets it right, but a professional practices until he can't get it wrong. That's the difference. And when they're not here, them players will still go on training runs." I asked him, "Who's the fittest one?" And he answered,

"Jack." "JACK?" "Yes, Jack, he jumps higher than any of them. In a match. And he can run all day." I said, "The Leeds fans have got to see this, they've got to see how fit the players are!" and he said, "They can see them in training here on Fullerton Park."

'I told him that I'd been in America and had watched the Cleveland Indians American football team in training and warm-ups, how everything was done in time, like it was all choreographed. It was amazing. So I said to Don that it would be good if the Leeds players could come out early before kick-off. Don queried this as, he said, the players came out before kick-off already, kicking a few balls about, and then the match starts. I said no, I think they should come out about 15 minutes earlier. Don said he couldn't work out what I was trying to do, he couldn't grasp it, what was I talking about?! I mentioned Busby Berkeley's old films, of the 1930s, and he had all these great routines, everyone in unison. Don didn't dismiss the idea but he definitely wasn't convinced either, so he told me to have a chat with Les, with a friendly warning as well – "If you went up to Les and mentioned Busby Berkeley he'd probably put one on you and chin you. He won't have it, you will never ever talk him into something like that."

'And so I went to talk to Les but he didn't seem to be really listening because he had his mind on other things. I asked if, on matchday, he could get the players out early before the kick-off so they could run around on the pitch and show the fans how fit they really were – "Les, the fans deserve to see what you've done, how you've driven the players to that level of fitness!" Not to put him down at all but Les very rarely laughed, and if you got a smile out him then you'd done well, but he said, "Let me think about it," with a pleasant enough look on his face. I thought, "That's a no then," as when people say let me think about it, it really means let me take my time before finally saying no. But he said it again, and that he'd need to talk to Don about it, so then I was thinking, "Brilliant, he's up for it!"

'He asked me when I was back up in Leeds again and to come and see him as he'd have something to show me, and that's when I realised I was talking to the artist Paul Gauguin who said, "I shut my eyes in order to see," because Les Cocker had seen, in that moment, what he was planning. *I* hadn't seen it! *Don* hadn't seen it! But Les had! He was talking to me and seeing it in his mind, he was seeing it and working it all out while we were standing there!

'I came back three days later and talked it through with Don, about the sock tags as well, and other things, and Don's saying things like, "Yes I like that … I like that … I'm not sure about that … I don't know about that," and adding that I'd convinced him but I'd have to see the players for the final word, I'd have to talk them into it. All I wanted was to see the players running around on the pitch before a match, showing the fans how super-fit they were, I didn't have any plan on how that could be done. But Les did, he did it, he did the business. He said to me, "Watch this," and the next minute, the players would be split up into six or four, and run to the four corners of the pitch. And it was precision, the different groups all arrived at the corner flags at the same time. And then they'd start to interchange, and I said to Les, "It's like watching the Red Arrows, not in the sky but on the ground," and Les laughed his head off, and that's possibly the only time I got a real laugh out of him, even though I wasn't joking. "But they're not red, Paul, they're white. Red's Man United and Liverpool."

The debut for the 'choreographed warm-ups' (as well as wearing the sock tags) came before the team's FA Cup quarter-final against Spurs at Elland Road. 'And the crowd,' Trevillion told me, 'went absolutely wild for it when the players did it for real. And that's when [journalist] Hunter Davies said how he couldn't believe how crazy the crowd went when seeing it for the very first time, he said it was like the Nuremberg hysteria, they loved it so much. It was an explosion of sound, an explosion, the ground literally shook! That wasn't my idea, my idea was just for the players to come out early, Les was the one who worked out all the routines and stuff. It blew me away, I'd never heard a sound like that at a football match before or since, ever, ever, ever, ever, even when Leeds scored that day! And the ground was packed, every single one in the ground seemed to be making a noise and going poppy, you've never heard a sound like it, I can tell you. And I've been to some big games and seen some very important goals go in, and never seen or heard anything like that.'

Trevillion had encountered Revie a few times over the years, starting in the 1950s at Professional Footballers' Association gatherings, long before he got to know Les. 'I met Don at PFA dinners in the 1950s – Don was always stood by the door as you walked in, so everyone who walked in, he'd shake their hand or welcome them in, so that meant every person knew that Don Revie was there. And Don Revie had the best laugh of anyone, an unbelievable laugh. He wanted to be liked! He'd always smile, he'd always be the approachable guy. You couldn't fall out with him. You could have a difference of opinion but you couldn't fall out with him, he wouldn't allow it.

'Les Cocker was more about wanting respect. He didn't mind if you liked him or not, just as long as you respected him. He wasn't in the football business looking for pats on the back, I can tell you that. He didn't want the praise and he wouldn't take it if you tried. But Les Cocker was one of the nicest guys you could wish to meet. Les Cocker told me himself, "I make the players do what they don't want to do, to turn them into the players that they want to be." Les was *the* man and I loved his philosophy: "No one's going to run faster than them, Paul. No one's going to bully them or push them off the ball."

'I saw the players sometimes looking at him like they wanted Les to ease off and give them a break, but he wasn't there to give them a break, he was there to make them better players. He was doing it for them! And if you look at photographs of them all on the pitch before the kick-off, there's one of them, one man, working harder and jumping higher than the rest, with his knees right up to his chest, and he doesn't have sock tags on, because that man is Les Cocker.

'At that time, that Leeds team would have beaten the Tottenham Double team, no question about it. Today, that Leeds team could give Man City a two goals start and still beat them, they were that good! They were the perfect blend, the perfect bloody blend, a team full of internationals! And that's what Les said to me, "You can teach technique but you can't teach talent. There's no coach in the world who can teach talent. They can teach technique, as in 'do this, do that' but no one can teach talent. These players have got it." Somehow, Don and Les and the fellas at Leeds had got together a group of brilliant lads who just wanted to play football. It wasn't about the money and the riches, they just wanted to play football and win, and they were always striving to be better.'

Paul Trevillion devised and illustrated pieces for nationals such as Daily Mirror, Daily Express, The Sun *and* The Daily Telegraph.

Trevillion had an appointment to get to, and so closed our conversation with this, 'Les Cocker was one of the nicest people I've ever met. Whatever he did, it wasn't for his own benefit, it was always to make the player or person better or fitter. He trained players hard for them, not for him!'

Here is part of the aforementioned Hunter Davies piece taken from his exceptional football memoir, 'The Leeds team had gone out first, in fact a good ten minutes before three o'clock, and were apparently causing a sensation. Their whole squad, 12 players and trainer Les Cocker, were in gleaming white tracksuit tops with their names printed large in blue on the back. It was the first time such a thing had been seen in the English First Division. On the outside of each stocking top hung the player's number, another innovation. But the biggest gimmick was their exercises. They ran in formation to the far corner of the pitch and started dancing in unison, high kicking, bending and jumping, all perfectly together and in time. They went round the pitch and performed to each section of the crowd in turn. They radiated confidence and fitness and the crowd went wild with excitement. When Spurs came out the boos were equally tremendous. At least at Liverpool, the home of crowd excitement, they'd managed a cheer for the visiting side. But the Leeds crowd were now in a state of almost Nuremberg hysteria … Whether it was the excitement of their callisthenics or their innate skills, Leeds played the first 20 minutes as if they really were footballing gods …'

The quarter-final was won 2-1 by Leeds, and those pre-match 'gimmicks' certainly helped add to the afternoon's excitement. Whether or not Trevillion's (and thus, Les's) involvement had any bearing on the actual football match and result is open for discussion, but the new attractions undeniably helped to crank up the Elland Road atmosphere and add to the entertainment value.

Cruel luck with injuries struck Leeds on Saturday, 8 April 1972, the week before the FA Cup semi-finals. In the afternoon, star left-back Terry Cooper suffered a broken leg in the first team away at Stoke City while, only hours earlier, versatile full-back Nigel Davey had fractured his leg in a reserve game against West Bromwich Albion. The FA Cup semi-final draw had paired Leeds with Birmingham City of the Second Division and though the underdogs produced a creditable display in the match, held at Hillsborough, they were comprehensively beaten 3-0. Leeds would meet holders Arsenal in the Wembley final, the Gunners having beaten Stoke in their semi-final after a replay. Years later, Davey told me, 'Don and Les, they'd just come over to the house with a big box of food and a load of fruit, and they sent over the biggest bunch of flowers every week for my wife Sandra. They had no real need to do that, but it's just how they were and how they cared for everyone at the club.'

Meanwhile, the First Division title race had been a superb contest all season, and among the league highlights for Leeds were the famous maulings of Manchester United and

Southampton, 5-1 and 7-0 respectively, as well as the less-celebrated 6-1 annihilation of Nottingham Forest and 5-1 win over Newcastle at Hillsborough during the Football League's four-match ban on playing at Elland Road. This epic saga saw four teams fight for the championship, culminating in Leeds having to play what effectively was the league title decider, two days after the FA Cup Final. Only the Football League of England seemed to think this was reasonable timing. The film *They Shoot Horses, Don't They?* sprang to mind, secretary Alan Hardaker in possession of the firearm.

Hardaker ruled the roost with an arrogance and stubbornness Napoleon would have admired. He clearly disliked Revie, particularly in regard to Revie's 'selfish' methods when, as Hardaker put it, 'He only wanted his team to play when, in his own mind, they were sure of winning,' which was, really, a silly comment to make. Was he really of the opinion that any professional football manager should choose to play matches at *disadvantageous* times? For balance, Revie was not alone in Hardaker's disdain and 'pain in the neck' stakes, he seemed to dislike all Football League managers, certainly the successful ones anyway. He did, though, reserve particular scorn for Revie, at one later stage accusing him of dishonesty and obsession with financial gain. Cheap, baseless jibes, and which were deeply, bitterly ironic considering serious claims of Hardaker's clandestine money siphoning and trousering.

The day before the Centenary FA Cup Final of Saturday, 6 May 1972, Revie told the press, 'Leeds United have an after-

Wembley banquet organised in a London hotel tonight but the players, trainer Les Cocker and myself will not be there. When our wives, directors, friends and other members of staff are sitting down to champagne and a massive nosh-up, we shall probably be calling in at a restaurant somewhere on the M1 for a cup of coffee and a snack.' This would turn out to be not entirely accurate.

Already, Trevillion's player sock tags had proved immensely popular, with modified (and cheaper-to-produce) versions also on sale at Elland Road and in selected retailers. For the final, special commemorative editions were made for the team and substitute, numbered one to 12, as well as tracksuit jackets which the coaching personnel were also provided with. Les looked perfect in his white jacket and blue bottoms. The players were supplied with two match shirts each as well, one long-sleeved and one short, though only captain Billy Bremner opted for the short sleeves. There were two unique versions, so to speak, of the sock tags: one showing 'Leeds v Arsenal Centenary FA Cup Final 1972' above the player's shirt number, and 'Leeds United A.F.C.' beneath, all in gold capitals. The other version omitted 'Leeds v Arsenal'. As was usually the case, Les was in charge of the kits and now the tags, too. In the Wembley dressing room he laid both sets of sock tags out and told the players to choose for themselves. He was also in charge of the Target footballs, ensuring each player walked out on to the Wembley pitch carrying a correspondingly numbered version; the balls would then be given (well, most of them were launched as the players emerged from the Wembley tunnel) to a few fortunate individuals in the crowd.

The quality of play in the final perhaps fell below the anticipated levels but it provided great intrigue and excitement, nonetheless; two prizefighters probing and testing each other. On balance, Leeds were the slicker and more incisive side but it was a close contest. The decisive moment came in the 53rd minute, Paul Madeley striding out of the Leeds defence with the ball before placing a pass to Peter Lorimer who advanced a few yards before supplying Mick Jones on the right channel of the pitch. Jones ventured forth, cleverly eluded Arsenal's Bob McNab and then struck a waist-high cross from the byline towards strike partner Allan Clarke near the penalty spot in Arsenal's area. Clarke launched himself in a spectacular dive and planted a powerful header to the left of Arsenal keeper Geoff Barnett into the corner of the net. Cue the immortal commentary, 'Clarke, 1-0!' and Leeds were on their way to winning the FA Cup for the first time. Commentary from David Coleman

Sadly, though, the drama wasn't over with as, in the last minute, Jones fell awkwardly after an innocent, winning challenge for the ball from Barnett on the edge of the six-yard box, close to the byline again. The whole incident seemed to be innocuous but Jones suddenly was in excruciating pain – he had put out his hand to break the fall but the arm had given way at the elbow – under his weight. He had sustained a sickening injury, dislocating the joint, and seconds passed before the extent of his problem was realised. Within the next 50 seconds, the referee had signalled the match was over and Leeds had won the FA Cup, while Les had sped to attend to the stricken Jones. Clearly, Les was deeply concerned with Jones's condition, and the situation was not being helped at all by a small crowd of well-meaning but infuriating people who had gathered there, including St John Ambulance men, reporters, and television and press cameramen. Even the marching band got too close.

Les, kneeling next to the prone player, gently attempted to ascertain the injury and keep Jones calm at the same time. It wasn't easy, and he gesticulated to everyone to stay clear of the patient, including Jack Charlton who had run across to check on his team-mate, and then substitute Mick Bates. An urgent voice can also be heard on certain TV footage demanding, 'Get the fucking doctor!' Within seconds, Dr Ian Adams was there but, really, Les had dealt with the situation more than adequately already. Other than tie a couple of long bandages around Jones's torso and left arm to keep the limb immobile and as comfortable as possible (*if* at all possible) there was nothing to be done at this stage.

In the meantime, the other Leeds players were in the process of climbing the Wembley steps to the Royal Box to receive their winners' medals from the Queen. Slowly, carefully, and assisted by Les and the doctor, Jones had reached the foot of the famous 39 steps; he was insisting on collecting his medal. Dr Adams began signalling to Norman Hunter to come and help. Jones, clearly in great pain, met the Queen, who asked how he was and graciously explained that she had no reward to give him (Mick Bates had already collected his medal on his behalf). But at least Jones had fulfilled his wish of meeting Her Majesty. Her husband, Prince Philip, looked rather concerned about Jones's welfare, while the Queen had other formal matters to consider.

As Jones slowly descended the steps at the other side of the Royal Box, and with the physical shock of the accident near overwhelming him, the national anthem commenced. The stadium was awash mainly in a sea of white, old gold and blue as the crowd sang. In the treatment room, it would be around an hour before the agonising procedure of re-placing Jones's elbow could be attempted, with four doctors including Dr Adams needed to hold him down, so intense was the pain.

That evening, while the Leeds players travelled to somewhere in the Midlands before Monday's crucial match with Wolverhampton Wanderers, Revie and Les were aboard the train back to Leeds – with the FA Cup. Dave Cocker tells me it was a Pullman train, the most luxurious rail service available, complete with waiter service onboard. Les rarely drank alcohol but it's likely he had a little taste of champagne from the Cup after Dave had ordered the bubbly from the bar, the tab the club's responsibility. Incidentally, dear reader, my mum and dad were on the train and were very happy to help with the champagne-supping, along with the few dozen others on the private charter.

From the wonder of the Wembley win, the Monday night game at Molineux descended into one of the most woeful days in Leeds' history. They lost 2-1 when a draw would have won the title and sealed the Double. Staging the match barely 52 hours after the FA's showpiece final was hard enough to understand or accept, and two blatant handballs in the Wolves penalty area not penalised by the referee were ridiculously bad decisions. And to think there had been allegations concerning attempted match-fixing by the club.

1972/73

For both of Les's employers, 1972/73 would prove rather gloomy, eventually leading to major upheaval for certain individuals. For England, qualification matches for the 1974 World Cup, to be held in West Germany, would begin, with 'preliminary' matches against their opponents in the three-team group – Wales and Poland – scheduled. As far as Les's workload went, the under-23s had seven matches to play to add to the full England team's 11. For Leeds, despite being in the top three for much of the season, their league form ultimately disappointed, a final position of third, seven points behind champions Liverpool and four behind Arsenal, convincing doubters that the players were approaching 'past it' stage. The results in two major cup finals did little to adjust the depressing views.

In September 1972, Leeds signed giant 20-year-old defender Gordon McQueen from St Mirren for around £30,000. McQueen came highly recommended by Tony Collins as the only centre-half in Britain with the potential to adequately replace Jack Charlton. Les, though, needed little introduction to McQueen as he was the son of former Accrington Stanley team-mate – and next-door neighbour – Tom McQueen, and good pals with son Dave.

Leeds' League Cup effort fizzled out with a 1-0 replay defeat at Elland Road to Liverpool in the fourth round, thanks to a very late Kevin Keegan header. With Leeds as the FA Cup holders, they had qualified for UEFA's European Cup Winners' Cup and would meet, en route to the final, teams from Turkey, East Germany, Romania and Yugoslavia. And the final, against one of Italy's most successful sides, AC Milan, would take place in Thessaloniki, Greece. The 1973 FA Cup campaign turned out to be a hard-fought slog for United, overcoming Norwich City, in the third round after two replays, Plymouth Argyle, West Bromwich Albion, Derby County at their Baseball Ground in the quarter-final, and Wolves at Maine Road in the semi-final where, incidentally, Les had to help hamstring-injured Jack Charlton off the pitch in the first half.

FA Cup Final, 5 May 1973

United suffered one of the greatest shocks in the competition's history, beaten 1-0 by Second Division Sunderland who certainly did not look a lower-league side on the day, and who had beaten Arsenal 2-1 in their semi-final. Leeds always expected a tough match but were strong favourites to win, though Paul Reaney later said that they had hoped to meet Arsenal in the final rather than Sunderland. Sunderland's victory was hard-earned and deserved.

Two nights later, Leeds hosted Celtic at Elland Road in the testimonial match for Jack Charlton; he had been with the club for over 23 years. Among the crowd of nearly 35,000 were Sean Connery, Jimmy Tarbuck and Michael Parkinson, all friends of Big Jack. Jack played in the match before being replaced by Gordon McQueen. Celtic won the entertaining game 4-3, and though Leeds had a league match to play two nights later, this fixture was heartily competed. Leeds would beat Arsenal 6-1, a marvellous boost for the following week's European final.

Charlton had already played his last competitive tie for Leeds and was leaving to take over as manager of Middlesbrough. Naturally, he was sad to be going after so many amazing years there, and he even briefly wept after the Celtic match, but there was a degree of bitterness too, towards the Leeds directors, as he explained in a subsequent memoir, 'They took £40,000 at the turnstiles on the night, which was a nice sum for a man who had never earned more than £175 a week. But then I saw the deductions – £12,000! What really bugged me was that they included a match fee of something like £8,000 to Celtic – and Celtic owed us a game for a match at Parkhead the previous year. Now, the Leeds directors could have insisted on a reciprocal arrangement and requested the Scots to scrap their fee for my game. But they didn't. Instead, they kept it for themselves, an asset to be cashed in at their time of choosing. I mean, it wasn't as if Leeds United was a poor club.'

European Cup Winners' Cup Final, 16 May 1973

At the Kaftanzoglio Stadium in Thessaloniki, Greece, even though Leeds were without key men through suspension and injury – Bremner, Clarke, Giles and Eddie Gray – the match sank into a most blatant example of a team being cheated. Greek referee Christos Michas was, tactfully speaking, 'rumoured' to have been bribed by Italian officials, and a Greek official too, possibly. He was later banned for life by UEFA. That is the same UEFA who chose the dishonest referee to officiate the match in the first place.

In his book, John Giles described how he had sustained an injury a few days before the meeting with AC Milan when playing for the Republic of Ireland in Moscow. It wasn't a serious injury but it was that most irritating kind, a hamstring strain. Giles had not been relishing the thought of informing Revie that he would have to miss the final, as the manager had broken down in front of everyone at the dinner following the FA Cup Final defeat to Sunderland. Giles, arriving alone at Leeds' Thessaloniki hotel base, said, 'When I got to the hotel, straight away I thought it as odd that Don wasn't there waiting to meet me – normally he would want to see how I was. He'd be anxious about any injuries I might have picked up on international duty, which was the bane of his life. Instead, Norman and Mick Bates were waiting for me. They looked anxious. But first, I went to find Les to tell him about my injury. He hardly reacted.'

The reason for Les's lack of reaction, perhaps indifference, to that news possibly was double-edged. Firstly, there were credible reports that the match was to be fixed in favour of the Italians. Secondly, Revie had unofficially accepted an invitation from Everton to be their new manager. Norman Hunter revealed the Everton rumour to Giles, and so they and Bates went to Revie's hotel room to ask him about it, 'Don was sitting on his bed – "Yes, I'm going" – and then, just as he had done at the Savoy, he broke down and cried.'

To the relief of the Leeds fans, with the possible exception of one or two directors in the Elland Road boardroom, Everton would pull out of the deal, fearing they might be charged by the Football Association for illegally approaching another club's manager.

Giles, being unavailable to play, was invited by the BBC to be a guest analyst for the match, and that was how he learnt, through the media, that the referee had been 'got at'. Peter Lorimer later wrote, 'It was wholly, indisputably and wretchedly bent,' while Paul Reaney, captain for the match, revealed, 'We were in the airport when the AC Milan plane landed. We were watching them as they came through ... Imagine our surprise when coming through with them was the referee Michas.'

It was alleged that the president of the Greek FA brokered the match-fixing deal with the referee, and that Artemio

Franchi, president of the Italian FA and newly anointed UEFA president too, with alleged mafia links also, was heavily involved. Of Franchi, writer Brian Glanville said, 'I always found Franchi to be a man who preferred to be honest, but given the nature of his own career in business and football, this was always going to be difficult.'

A few days after the final, UEFA banned referee Michas for life. Leeds were not alone in dubious dubious, suspicious events seeming to conspire against them. Other English teams, including Derby and Liverpool, also had occasions of feeling distinctly hard done by, by referees who might well have been 'got at' – or been, as Clough said after a Derby defeat to Juventus, 'cheating bastards'. Ten years later Franchi died in a 'a supposedly straightforward' car crash in Italy, in 1983. Corruption in European football continued without him. For example, Nottingham Forest's UEFA Cup semi-final versus Anderlecht was proved to be rigged in favour of the Belgian side.

* * *

After a disastrous 2-0 World Cup qualifying match defeat in Katowice to Poland on 6 June, with the refereeing performance described by irritated English pressmen as 'one of the worst ever seen', England's senior team had a brace of friendlies to play, in Russia and Italy. Dr Neil Phillips was still an important part of the set-up, as was Les. Dr Phillips wrote, 'Prior to the game v Russia, the British Embassy in Moscow were keen for the England players to develop good relations with the Russian public. They had arranged for the entire party to pay their respects to Lenin at his tomb in Red Square. We all assembled mid-morning in the searing heat of a June day, dressed in our official suits. The British Embassy staff greeted us on arrival. The queue of public waiting to pay their respects to Lenin was huge. Embassy staff tried to negotiate for us to get to the front of the queue. It took about 30 minutes and the players were getting agitated in the heat.

'Another ten minutes and we were told the negotiations had failed, a senior Russian officer refused to allow our party to jump the queue. The officer told the players to return to the hotel. They began to depart but a soldier was over-keen to see immediate exit and, approaching Les Cocker and myself, Les lost his temper and stood face to face with the soldier, "My uncle Charlie is buried in Stockport cemetery, I wouldn't even queue up to see him and he was a better man than Lenin!"'

On 10 June 1973, in stiflingly humid conditions, England played well and beat Russia 2-1. Stoke City left-back Mike Pejic was a member of the squad at the time but would gain his first cap the following year. He recalled that the pressure on Sir Alf Ramsey's role as manager was increasing. Much of that pressure came from within the FA, where Ramsey had few influential allies, despite his achievements with the national side. Pejic mentioned an incident while in Russia, 'We were on the coach waiting for some of the FA officials who were still hanging around the hotel. Alf sent Les Cocker inside with the instruction to tell the FA men that, "If you are not on the bus in two minutes then you're going to have to catch taxis." Next thing you saw the FA officials running down the steps and racing each other to get on the bus. Alf was really about to say, "Off we go." It was one of the sort of things that probably cost him in the end.'

Four days following the Russia win, England went down 2-0 to Italy in Turin, the match commemorating the 75th anniversary of the formation of the Italian FA. England played well in the first half without seriously threatening Italy's goal too much. The English media's pressure on Ramsey was slowly building, and while his relationship with the press had never been the warmest, he did at least make himself available for interviews and quite intense scrutiny. One specific question particularly caught the attention, in the *Daily Mirror* from respected journalist Ken Jones, 'The defeat in Italy underlined long-standing technical deficiencies and the contrast in style resurrected the fear that England are running short of top-class players. Derby manager Brian Clough, who criticised you recently, said that as England manager you had 2,000 players to pick from.' Ramsey's response was revealing, 'Rubbish. For obvious reasons you have to discount most of the players in the Second, Third and Fourth Divisions. That leaves you with around 230 players playing regularly for First Division clubs. Take away the Scots, the Irish, the Welsh and the Eire players and you are cutting the figure down by about 60. Of those who are left, some are too old for international football and others don't quite come up to standard. The England manager, whoever he is, is really working with about forty or so players.'

On 17 October 1973, Ramsey's England were at home against Poland in their closing World Cup 1974 qualifier. England had to win to progress to the finals; nothing else would do. With more than 30 shots on goal compared to Poland's two, England, quite incredibly, blew it, only drawing 1-1 thanks to stupendous defending and goalkeeping from the Poles. The 1966 world champions wouldn't be going to the 1974 World Cup.

9

1974 and past it?

MORE FROM John Giles about Les Cocker, 'Les as a person was a top-notcher. He did his job perfectly and was dedicated to what he was doing. Socially we weren't that close as he was on the staff and it's not the right way to do it, to get too close to the players when you're on the staff. We were all together and close as a group in the professional sense, going in the same direction, and you absolutely could trust him and confide in him.'

Not quite 33 years old and still an integral part of the Ireland first 11, Giles took a huge step in his career by becoming player-manager of his country's team in October 1973. I enquired, did Don Revie and Les influence him at all?

'Well of course, but everybody has their own ideas and their own different ways of doing things, but there is always something you can learn from others. First of all, Don's way was always "honesty of effort". Everybody had to give their effort, no messing about as we were a team and we all played for each other. And that's the way it should be done, it's a basic, regardless of team ability and tactics which is very overrated, to be quite honest. Don got some terrific players in of course but the basis was always – when you get out on that pitch then you're doing the very best that you can, for the team. That was the big thing for Don and that doesn't happen overnight, you have to get the right players in.

'But international football was a totally different game to club football. My first match as manager of the international team was on a Sunday, and with no preparation because there was no time at all then to prepare with the international team. Particularly in those days as we were with our club teams just about every day, and there was no time off for players then in time for an international. You just had to accept it as it was, but you learn as you go along, this is how to do things, and I had a good education, first with Matt Busby and then under Don. But you have to do things your own way. And Les and Don were very good to me – for my first international match, Leeds were playing Liverpool on the Saturday but I was injured so couldn't play. The Ireland match was on Sunday and Don let me go on the Friday and he even let Les come away a little bit early to help me in my first international match in charge. Les was somebody that I could trust, that I could bring to Ireland and I knew he would do the job that was needed to be done. Very, very professional and good at his job. This was a one-off, it wouldn't have been fair of me to ask again but as this was my first match …'

Four days after their draw with England at Wembley to end English hopes of qualification to the 1974 World Cup finals, Poland were beaten 1-0 in a friendly against Giles's Republic of Ireland.

In two friendlies, England narrowly lost to Italy in November at Wembley and drew 0-0 with Portugal in Lisbon on 3 April 1974. By the end of April, Sir Alf Ramsey had been sacked as England manager, six months after that fateful qualifier match with Poland. His uneasy relationship with FA officials was well-known of course and, as sure as (bad) eggs is (bad) eggs, there were long-held grudges against him by certain individuals in the ivory towers of Lancaster Gate. Indisputably at the top of that list was an obnoxious high-up nicknamed, secretly, by some as 'the groper'. Renowned writer Leo McKinstry also said, of Ramsey's exit, 'England's most successful manager would have had a legacy fit for a hero had it not been for the malevolence of the FA chief Harold Thompson.' Joe Mercer would be made England's interim manager, for seven matches, while the FA found a replacement for Ramsey.

On hearing the news of Sir Alf's dismissal, Les telephoned his good friend and colleague Dr Neil Phillips. Apparently, no decision had been made as to who would succeed Ramsey and manage England for the close season Home Internationals, a friendly against Argentina and a scheduled tour of East Germany, Bulgaria and Yugoslavia. Les expressed his disgust at the FA's decision, calling the sacking a 'bloody disgrace' and vowing to not go on the tour, adding that they could 'stuff it'. Dr Phillips agreed, saying, 'Like you, if Alf is sacked, so am I. I'll let you know if I hear anything.' Ramsey's other lieutenant, Harold Shepherdson, also concurred with Phillips and Cocker's sentiments. No surprise there, a sign of their loyalty to their friend and 'gaffer'. Dave Cocker said that his dad telephoned Ramsey soon after to tell him that, in a show of solidarity, he would be resigning his post as England trainer due to the FA's disgraceful behaviour. Ramsey appreciated the gesture but he told Les that absolutely no one should resign, he did not want anything of the sort to happen.

Aware of the resentment among Ramsey's staff caused by the quite brutal sacking, Ted Croker, the new FA secretary recruited in 1973 as successor to retiree Denis Follows, asked for a meeting with Phillips, Cocker and Shepherdson, in an effort to clear the air and try to mend bridges. Dr Phillips wrote about Les's angry response, referring to the England 1966 table mats rebuff, 'In my book, every member of staff and every player should have had a set. I'll tell him what's wrong ... first rule, value your staff and your players. The FA should realise the players and staff are more important than the officials.'

Mercer was a popular chap. A generally cheerful and sociable man, he had a managerial style which could be described as 'relaxed'. This might well have been connected to his suffering a stroke in 1964 while Aston Villa boss, after a stressful season fighting against relegation. The team won that battle but Mercer, after his recovery, would be sacked anyway. His next managerial role was with Manchester City, starting in 1965. Mercer worked a virtual miracle there, gaining promotion to the First Division and then advancing to win major trophies with his exciting team, helped by Malcolm Allison as his assistant. A takeover of the club, involving Allison, caused things to sour at Maine Road, and Mercer was ostensibly pushed out. He became manager of Coventry City in 1972, and now he was England's caretaker manager. He appeared to be a popular choice with players and the media alike.

When Mercer took charge, there were no objections from Les, Dr Phillips or Shepherdson, they were friends and colleagues and their mutual aims were to improve England matters and establish them again as a world force. How they went about accomplishing those aims might be another story, they were individuals possessing individual ideas and plans. From the beginning, Les advised Mercer that he shouldn't be too blasé or relaxed with the England players, they needed to remain disciplined and professional, England's standards should not be allowed to drop with a change of manager. However, Mercer was of the opinion that Ramsey had been too strict with the players and for too long. Mercer had decided that he wanted to relax things in the England set-up a little. Les warned him that it would be problematic, the England team's on-field woes and poor results had nothing to do with off-field strictness and 'code of conduct'.

It seemed Les's thoughts on the matter were ignored, with Mercer allowing the players to travel in casual attire, without official England blazers. England's Eastern Europe tour was treated like a break by some, rather than a serious, professional series of engagements. The players took advantage of the new regime, dressing, it was said, 'like hippies' and acting 'like they were in a rock group'. Some of them *were* like rock stars, B-list perhaps but, still, famous in British culture. Alas, few people outside of Britain would have heard of them, and any 'high jinks' behaviour from them would have been, effectively, asking for trouble when on foreign land.

Having drawn 1-1 with East Germany and then winning 1-0 against Bulgaria in what Mercer described as a 'great victory', the last friendly of the tour was to be in Yugoslavia. On the flight from Sofia to Belgrade, Mercer, Dr Phillips, Shepherdson and Les sat at the rear of the aeroplane. A few members of the FA hierarchy sat nearby, and the entire playing squad occupied seats a few rows in front. Footballers and FA 'suits', drinking, sharing the same space, but probably only equals in their lack of sobriety. There had been, it was alleged, a common ruse among England players to get 'over-familiar' with stewardesses while on flights, without conferring with the stewardesses. On this particular flight, one stewardess was 'goosed' by an unnamed individual. One player certainly innocent of such grubby behaviour was Kevin Keegan, who was asleep on the flight. Regardless, the stewardess reported the matter to the aircraft captain who then radio-relayed the matter to the Belgrade Airport authorities.

Inside Belgrade Airport, Liverpool left-back Alec Lindsay was clowning around, struggling to prise his luggage from the carousel. Emlyn Hughes and Frank Worthington were enjoying the spectacle too, and helped to add to the comedy. Keegan was an amused spectator, sitting innocently on the edge of the belt, watching and laughing. Unfortunately for him, he was being watched and was about to be singled out for 'special attention' by annoyed officers. He was marched away to a private room before any of his team-mates could react or object, and then he was treated to a very unwelcome and very painful Belgrade reception. In the private room he was forced to kneel 'like a prisoner of war' and was punched, clubbed and kicked. And then he was charged with sexually assaulting the air stewardess, assaulting a security guard, disturbing the peace and causing an obstruction.

1973/74

Leeds had started the league season like a juggernaut, winning seven games on the trot, their first dropped point coming in a surprise 0-0 home draw with Manchester United. Their first defeat didn't come until February 1974, after a run of 29 games unbeaten. And they had achieved it with real panache. That first reverse though – at Stoke City – famously or infamously, depending on your loyalties, came after Leeds had been 2-0 up, and prompted a bout of the jitters followed by just one win in their next six. Second-placed Liverpool were let back into the hunt again. In the FA Cup, another giant-killing occurred, deservedly, to quote Revie, in the fifth-round replay against Bristol City. On Tuesday, 19 February – in the afternoon due to government-imposed power cuts – City won 1-0.

One week before the barely respectful ridding of Ramsey, Revie was the unsuspecting subject of the ITV production *This Is Your Life*, a show regularly watched by millions of viewers in the UK. Leeds had beaten Ipswich at Elland Road the preceding Saturday while main title challengers Liverpool had dropped a point against Everton and then lost at home to Arsenal, leaving them five points behind with only four left to play for. After the TV programme had been aired, the same night as Liverpool's defeat, Les joked, 'It has been a grand week for Don – the championship, a great match last Saturday, *This Is Your Life*, and he even beat Val Doonican at golf.'

The Revie edition of the famous tribute programme was filmed at the Queens Hotel in Leeds, a real Art Deco landmark of the city, where he had been expecting to be attending a sportsmen's dinner event. Instead, he received a shock, to be pounced on by presenter Eamonn Andrews in front of the television cameras. Famous personalities in the audience included Joe Mercer, Michael Parkinson, Colin Welland, Harvey Smith and Freddie Trueman, among many others. Guest interviewees speaking in Revie's honour included Bill Shankly and Sir Matt Busby, as well as Leeds captain Billy Bremner.

With respect to who would be chosen as Ramsey's permanent successor as England manager, there were several names spoken of in the media and football circles. But Revie, to the dismay of Leeds fans, was favourite to be offered the job. That said, Les, for instance, urged him not to take it as it was the worst international squad Les had known in his career; there were too many 'ordinary' players around when the hard truth was that England were in dire need of dedicated, determined and 'extraordinary' players. Revie, after asking Tony Collins's opinion, discovered that Les was not on his own with this view. Collins had answered the question with a question of his own, 'Do you really know what you're doing, Don?' Revie asked what he meant, and Collins answered, 'Well, in my opinion, the England team are simply not good enough at the moment and if you take this job, you may be on a hiding to nothing – and it could go badly for you!' Revie replied, 'You may well be right, Tony, but let me ask you this – how on earth can I really refuse?'

By 5 July it had been confirmed. Revie was the new England manager. Bearing in mind that his Leeds team had won the First Division again, it was hardly a case of Revie abandoning the club in a time of need. Nonetheless, he wanted only the best for the club and, with that in mind, he recommended to the board of directors, chaired by Manny Cussins, that John Giles be his successor. That way, in Revie's considered, sincere opinion, he would be leaving the club in good hands and with minimal disruption to the overall playing and coaching structure. Indeed, it is reliably reported that Giles had spoken with Cussins and a verbal understanding reached that he would be the new boss, possibly with Les as his assistant (though that specific matter had not been discussed).

However, in a quite astounding development which exposed Cussins's lack of courage in his own convictions and suggested he had meekly ceded authority, the job 'offer' to Giles was rescinded; Cussins had been overruled by one, possibly two resentful directors unappreciative of Revie's advice. One of the men was Bob Roberts, who had contributed hugely to the costs of renovating Elland Road. He had gained much power and sway in the boardroom too, the club financially indebted to him for years. Roberts was not a particular fan of Revie or Les and once Revie had resigned, he saw the opportunity to show the world of football what he could do with 'his' club. After all, how dare a gifted, proven, hugely successful manager such as Revie, instrumental in putting Leeds well and truly on the map of world football, have the gall to make such suggestion to such bastions of English football (boardrooms)?! And poor Giles had been turned down for a job that he hadn't even applied for.

Brian Clough would be the new manager of Leeds. Clough officially took charge at Elland Road on 31 July 1974. On the same day, Les announced his resignation. Les was joining Revie again, now as his assistant manager for England. Clough would be gone from Elland Road after 44 days of bad feeling and bad management. After he had departed, with a spectacular financial exit package in his coffers, Cussins offered the manager's job to Giles again. Giles told the club, 'Stick your job offer up your ... jumper!'

Les had asked to see the board at the next meeting, a Monday night, ostensibly to sign off and say his farewells; he had been with the club for 14 years. They had agreed the time, 8pm. Les got there early, as was his custom for any appointment, and sat outside the boardroom for over an hour. When the directors finally came out and acknowledged his presence, the message conveyed to him was, 'Sorry, we haven't time to see you.' Les was well aware that this discourtesy had been instigated by Roberts, and Clough was 'his man' too. When Clough was to be sacked, Roberts was said to have gone on holiday, leaving Cussins to deal with all the mess.

On the England front, early in Revie's tenure, Tony Collins became a scout of sorts for the national side, monitoring match performances of England's players and opponents. He would become affectionately known as 'football's master spy', though he had been analysing player strengths and weaknesses, utilising the notorious dossiers, for quite some time already.

10

Two eras

IN AUGUST 1974, with Les Cocker instrumental in the situation, Don Revie invited Fulham coach Bill Taylor to the England fold. Second Division Fulham, managed by Alec Stock, had forged a good reputation as a most attractive, attacking side, a reflection on Edinburgh-born Taylor's approach to the game. In an interview about the England role, he said, 'Managers and coaches who advocate the modern defensive systems have no right to be in football. They should be kicked out for the damage they have done both to the entertainment value and to young players with skill and flair who are told it is a crime to take players on. England have as many, if not more, skilful players as they have on the continent but they are being stifled by these defensive tactics.'

During the 1974 World Cup in Germany, Taylor and another of Fulham's coaching staff were offered accommodation in Frankfurt. He said, 'The first person I met over there was Les Cocker. He was having coffee with commentator John

Motson, who introduced us. We chatted and Les seemed to take an interest. He tried to look after us as we were not very well-organised with things like travel arrangements.'

Taylor thought little more of the matter until the end of August 1974 when the job offer arrived; he wasn't completely sure it was genuine, 'I was in a whirl for ten days and still thinking that at any moment the phone would ring and someone would confirm that it was all a joke. When it did sink in I realised what a fabulous opportunity was opening up before me. It was recognition I had never received in my career before. What pleased me most was that I had never been an international or even top-class professional and they are the ones who are always considered first for the top managerial and coaching jobs, even though they seldom turn out to be the right people. They have never been put in the third team, dropped, or been six weeks on the substitutes' bench. That is the first sort of thing you must go through before you can understand what some players in your club have to suffer.'

England 1974/1975

Although it took over 70 minutes to register their first goal, Revie's England reign started brightly in the European Championship qualifier against Czechoslovakia at Wembley on 30 October. Wearing a new kit supplied by Admiral, England won 3-0. For now, any sceptics – and there would 'naturally' be many before long – decided on discretion rather than diatribe, almost as if they were keeping their gunpowder dry, or their poison preserved, for any future combat. After the match, in what would be affectionately called the Don Revie Suite, there was a party mood on the tenth floor of the Esso Hotel, close to Wembley Stadium. England players, management and officials were there, along with specially invited friends, too, including famous fans and most English First Division club managers. And, as always, pop star Elton John was present, England's number one celebrity fan as well. Other celebrities there included Rick Wakeman, Eric Clapton, Eric Morecambe, and music manager John Reid.

Precisely three weeks after England's impressive win over the Czechs, their second Euro qualifier, at home to Portugal, ended in a dour 0-0 draw, and the hot seat was suddenly increasing in temperature beneath Revie. Between the two matches, some critics had enjoyed mocking the officially organised gathering of English players at Manchester's Piccadilly Hotel, on the evening of Saturday, 21 September. Revie and his assistant Les had greeted all the invited players individually in the hotel foyer, shaking them by the hand as they arrived from their league matches around the country; 91 players in all, including a very few from the Second Division and one from the Third Division. They were there for a kind of open day, a clarion call almost, for the future of England as a major football power. The players had had to make their own way there, and they would have to make their own way back home too, the following day. That was one aspect Revie intended to change. In future, for any England matches or meetings, private cars or taxis would be used to collect the players and take them to the venue, and they would be driven home afterwards too. Dave Cocker, by now 23, enjoyed fast driving and was relishing the prospect of being one of the selected drivers, for northern-based players. He would have Revie's Jaguar XJ12 at his disposal too.

With Les's Leeds commitments no more, one would think his travels would have experienced a radical reduction, but in fact he and Revie were still driving over 700 miles a week each, travelling to matches to monitor players and then report on their progress. Those reports were written in similar style to the dossiers so often used by Leeds, especially in the 1960s when analysing opposing teams or transfer targets. They would be typed out by Revie's faithful secretary, Jean Reid, who had joined England from Leeds as well. Les drove his own car, his red Saab – the red of England's St George's Cross – with the FA meant to pay his petrol money, though it was usually a chore for Les to actually arrange the reimbursement. Revie's vehicle was a 'company' car, the lilac Jaguar XJ12.

In late November, a rare press interview with Les was published, 'Long after the jeering fans had left Wembley and the Portuguese had celebrated their 0-0 draw with England, manager Don Revie found a shoulder to cry on. The shoulder has been a vital crutch to Revie during his years of management. It has soaked up the tears and taken the slaps of joy as the man it belongs to, chief coach Les Cocker, has shared the mixed emotions that management brings. He is content in his role. Happy to be in the shadows of the man he admires above all others, untroubled that the glory rarely rubs off but knowing he is as important to Don Revie as Ernie Wise is to Eric Morecambe.

'Les Cocker should have made it on his own. Everyone in football respects his deep knowledge of the fame, his training methods and his own super fitness which set an example to players 20 and more years his junior. But when the offers came, he turned them down to stay with Revie. "I will stay in Don Revie's shadow," he said, contentedly puffing on his pipe. "There's a lot of people who would give anything to be in the same position. What have I got to achieve by leaving him unless it was a better job that was offered? I don't think I could find a better job than under him. Oh yes, I've had offers. When Don left to take the England job, a First Division and Second Division club came in for me. I wasn't interested." His devotion to Revie is unshakable.

'So close is their relationship that Cocker knew exactly what Revie would say after the disappointment v Portugal. He has heard it before, after defeats by Sunderland, Bristol City and Colchester. "I have always wondered at him after results like this. He is pig-sick yet he has kept it to himself. Don never minded losing if his team played football. It was when they lost and didn't play, like v Sunderland, that really hurt him. He would always say the same words, 'Well pal, we've got to pick 'em up off the floor again. Don't be too hard on them,' then he would pick them up himself without them knowing it and they would go and die for him in the next game."

'Only Cocker knows how Revie suffered in his last 12 months at Leeds. "During that time it would never have surprised me to see him go. People were fighting Don from within the club … can you imagine it, after all he had done, fighting him? I saw him in tears many times and it severely damaged his health." During this period Cocker was ready to walk out on the England trainer's job he had enjoyed for 13 years because he didn't like the way things were going. He would have quit if someone had not taken him to one side and predicted that Revie would be offered the job. It gave them both a new lease of life. "Don's a changed man," he said with a smile. "His eyes are sparkling again, it is a job he always wanted to do, managing England. Don had a marvellous team at Leeds but he was always saying, 'If I were manager of England I'd do this,' working with different people, the challenge … he would have been unhappy if he had missed it. The one thing he will always regret is that he never guided his Leeds team to the European Cup. That was the one he wanted above all others and it was the only thing which could have stopped him taking the England job." Don Revie will have to be content in going for the World Cup instead. That is his object now and as a winner he will expect to win it. If he does, expect to see little Les Cocker standing there beside him and out of the shadows.'

TWO ERAS

England 'bounced' back from November's disappointing draw, although 'bounce' is hardly the appropriate term for the next match taking place nearly four months later. And therein lay one of Revie's bigger problems in managing a national team rather than a club side: the lack of regular matches and meetings and teamwork, the absence of the spirit of family, community and camaraderie. He had worked so hard to establish such vital ingredients at Leeds, where the band of brothers had regarded Revie as the father figure, and Les as a favourite uncle, which was practically impossible to replicate for England. Recreating such wonderful alchemy was a romantic but implausible idea at international level. And it was a great shame for Revie, Cocker, the players and English football in general.

On 12 March 1975, England beat West Germany 2-0 in a Wembley friendly commemorating the 100th international match held there. It was a fine result and the Germans' first defeat since winning the World Cup the previous year.

The following month they beat Cyprus 5-0 at Wembley in another European Championship qualifier. Malcolm Macdonald scored all five goals in a splendid display, though England really ought to have scored more and, in untypically modest fashion, Macdonald admitted that he should have scored eight in total as he missed three fairly easy chances. It was a decent scoreline but there was, already, an uneasy feeling that five goals against such a weak team would prove inadequate. Such matters only worsened in the return tie a month later. A 1-0 win in Cyprus on 11 May was played on an atrociously dry and bumpy pitch. It was dour and uninspiring, but a win nonetheless.

The Home Internationals followed, and a goalless draw on 17 May with Northern Ireland followed by a 2-2 in Wales four days later hardly improved the outlook, but then a fabulous win over Scotland at Wembley on 24 May excited everyone. It was a magnificent display all round from Revie's England as they trounced Scotland 5-1.

Meanwhile, Leeds had experienced a turbulent season, Jimmy Armfield succeeding Brian Clough as manager, and with a huge task in despite the team being reigning league champions. One major challenge facing Armfield was the number of players coming to the end of their contracts; should he offer them new deals or invite approaches from other clubs for their services? To what degree he successfully dealt with particular situations will always be a matter of conjecture, but he deserved credit for trying to manage the club tactfully and calmly, after the board of directors and Clough had caused so much unnecessary upheaval. Les knew Armfield well from their England days in the early to mid-1960s, Les as trainer and Jimmy as a good right-back and member of the 1966 World Cup-winning squad.

Leeds struggled in the 1974/75 First Division and had suffered an ignominious exit from the League Cup to lowly Chester. The FA Cup campaign was a significantly better effort but, after an epic quarter-final against Ipswich Town which had needed three replays, that also ended in defeat.

There had been the slightly embarrassing failure to beat non-league Wimbledon at the first attempt in the fourth round, too. Great for the neutrals to see and for the 'romance' of the FA Cup. The shining beacon for Leeds' season was the European Cup, with the team progressing to their first final in the competition. Not that Armfield was the type to try and take credit for the achievement, instead crediting the players' endeavours for getting them there.

On 28 May 1975, the European Cup Final between Leeds and Bayern Munich was played at the Parc des Princes stadium in Paris, France. Revie and Les, two of the most important figures in the club's history, were not invited by the club to attend the final. What classy, respectful behaviour from the directors. Revie attended, as he was the main pundit for the BBC's TV coverage. Les did not obtain a ticket so did not go to the match. Leeds' secretary at the time, Keith Archer, wrote to Les to apologise for the discourtesy displayed by the board. Archer had been with the club since the mid-1960s, had been an important part of the United 'family' and knew how to treat people with respect, especially someone as influential and loyal to Leeds as Les.

As to the final itself, the less said the better really. Leeds were the better team on the night but the records show that Munich won, helped by a repugnant refereeing performance. Many in football believe that the match was another scandalous fix. Judging by Michel Kitabdjian's diabolical officiating, and with Artemio Franchi on the board of UEFA, anything and everything murky was entirely plausible. For example, two Herculean-strong claims for Leeds penalties were ludicrously dismissed by the referee, and after he and his linesman initially allowed Lorimer's fantastic goal, he changed his mind moments later.

England 1975/76

For a 2-1 friendly win in Switzerland on 3 September, Revie decided that the England players should wear different shirt numbers to normal in an attempt to confuse watching Czech officials checking on the team's form in time for their match in two months' time. The ploy probably had zero effect.

England would lose that qualifier 2-1, a crucial result which seriously damaged their hopes of progressing to the quarter-final stage. The Czechs probably deserved the win but physically battered England throughout, often illegally, their cause helped by weak refereeing.

England's final qualifier, on 19 November, saw them draw 1-1 in Portugal. They went a goal down on 16 minutes and were fortunate to not lose. The draw left the Czechs needing just one point in Cyprus to qualify ahead of England; they beat the Cypriots in a canter and went on to win the European Championship. That was no consolation whatsoever to Revie, whose team had failed and he was, for many, culpable for the failure.

On 24 March 1976, England beat Wales 2-1 away in a friendly marking the FA of Wales Centenary. Crystal Palace's

Peter Taylor became the first Third Division player to be capped for England since Johnny Byrne in 1961. Taylor came on as substitute for Mick Channon and scored the victory-clinching second goal ten minutes from the end.

Wales were again beaten on their own turf, this time 1-0 on 8 May, in the Home Internationals. England were fortunate not to be three down before Taylor scored the only goal of a scrappy match. Exceptional goalkeeping by Clemence saved England from defeat.

Mick Channon, dropped against Wales, responded with a notable performance in which he scored twice in a 4-1 home win over Northern Ireland three days later, then Scotland beat England 2-1 on 15 May. Ray Clemence undid his good work against Wales when a poorly struck shot from Kenny Dalglish rolled through his legs for Scotland's winning goal. Channon had given England an 11th-minute lead only for Bruce Rioch to equalise soon after, heading in an Eddie Gray corner past Clemence.

Next up was the USA Bicentennial Soccer Cup, arranged to celebrate the 200th anniversary of the USA's Declaration of Independence. England and Italy had both failed to qualify for the 1976 European Championship and so joined Brazil and Team America to compete. The real USA team of the time was not developed enough to compete against sides as powerful as Brazil, Italy and England, so 'Team America' was formed, consisting of players of various nationalities from North American Soccer League clubs.

On 23 May, England were beaten 1-0 by Brazil. Any match against Brazil was considered a big deal for England, even if their opponents were inferior compared to their greats of 1970. A last-minute goal by substitute Roberto gave Brazil a flattering victory, England having dominated much of the match. 'It was heartbreaking to lose so late in the game,' commented Revie. Many agreed, recognising a good England performance and fair degree of honour in the defeat.

England's next match saw them go two goals down to Italy inside the first 20 minutes, but they struck back to win with three goals in the opening seven minutes after the break. The game was played on a poor-standard surface, a baseball pitch more used to hosting the New York Yankees. The quality of play was of a good standard nonetheless. Channon was in inspiring form as captain, and his two goals sandwiched a headed goal by Phil Thompson. Even when Italy were 2-0 up, their players seemed more intent on attacking England's players rather than their goal. Even Italy's substitutes got involved, Trevor Cherry being spat at while warming up near their dugout. Les had experienced countless unsavoury incidents in his career but this was one of the worst. He kept his cool though, not descending to the Italians' base level of behaviour. Revie remarked that it was the worst behaviour he had ever seen in his whole career.

Manchester City goalkeeper Joe Corrigan, one of England's substitutes, later wrote, 'We went in 2-0 down at the break and me and a few of the other substitutes went out for a kick around to sample the atmosphere and keep ourselves warmed up. Then coach Les Cocker ran across to me – "You'd better come back in Joe, you're playing." I thought he was joking and told him as much ... I jogged back in to find Don Revie waiting – "Get ready, you're going on now, son."' Corrigan replaced Jimmy Rimmer, who had not looked at all comfortable in his first, and last, England match.

England's final match of the tournament came on 21 May as they beat Team America 3-1. With their opponents not a recognised national side, the FA ranked this match as a training game rather than a full international and therefore no caps were awarded to the England players. Understandable, though funnily enough both Brazil and Italy's associations classified their matches against Team America as full internationals. America's team included some surprise names, such as Pelé, Mike England, Tommy Smith, Giorgio Chinaglia, Dave Clements and former England captain and legend Bobby Moore. Moore wasn't even ticked off for this terrible act of treachery. England's win left them in second place behind Brazil in the competition.

Within two weeks of the tour, England were back to more serious football and the important matter of the 1978 World Cup qualification campaign, beginning with a 4-1 win against Finland in Helsinki.

Kevin Keegan was outstanding as England got off to a flying start. The only downside of the performance was that

England missed easy chances against the second-weakest team in the qualification group, and goal difference had the potential to be significant in a group also containing Italy and Luxembourg. The squad had been together for over a month. In his autobiography, Phil Thompson wrote, 'Don Revie had promised us that if we abstained from drinking any alcohol in the preparations for the match, he would ensure we had a sensational party afterwards after being together so long. He didn't let us down. After the game we all went down to this big restaurant-cum-nightclub where there was this electric organ. I remember that all the tables had "Reserved" on them. Elton John's manager John Reid gave the manager hell, pointing out that we were legends in England. Ray Wilkins was up dancing on the tables. Good old Elton got up on stage and gave us all his hits. Peter Taylor, who had a decent voice, sang with him on a few. The whole squad almost drank the place dry. Elton picked up the tab.' Alas, the Finland win was probably the last real highlight of Revie and Les's England association.

England 1976/77

In a way similar to a football version of the master versus the apprentice, John Giles's Republic of Ireland team were unlucky not to win their friendly against Revie's England at Wembley in September 1976, drawing 1-1.

The second qualifier against Finland came next, England recording a narrow and unsatisfying 2-1 win. The team had struggled to break through the stubborn Finnish defensive line but really they had no good excuses, it had been a poor display and the notoriously fickle England fans had turned against them. Their disgruntlement was somewhat justified with England's next match, the first qualifier against Italy, in Rome, in November. Revie did not seem to know what his best side was, perhaps most clearly demonstrated by selecting Stan Bowles in midfield. Italy won too easily, 2-0, and England's qualifying hopes were in tatters. Another 2-0 defeat followed, albeit in a friendly, to the Netherlands at Wembley in February 1977. England were embarrassed and humbled by a superb Johan Cruyff-inspired performance, the hosts 'chasing shadows' for much of the time.

On 30 March, England hosted Luxembourg in the World Cup qualifier. England won 5-0, with four goals in the last half hour, providing a more respectable scoreline. Realistically speaking, for England to have a good chance of reaching the finals in Argentina, it was felt they needed at least an eight-goal margin against Luxembourg. Finland had beaten Luxembourg 7-1, so it stood to reason that England should be able to better that score. Sadly, as the match progressed, it never looked likely, with the players too anxious and too predictable in their attacks. Next up on the pitch for England would be the Home Internationals in late May and early June.

Les knew Revie better than anyone else in football did, acknowledging that he was 'his own man' and that his standards had always been set high. In Les's experience, Revie had always been single-minded in his team selections, regardless of any misgivings from others, and rarely, if ever, asked for others' opinions. But by the autumn of 1976, it seemed clear that his confidence and courage of his own convictions had slipped; he now seemed to be unsure of his preferred first 11 and was even taking notice of media comment on who should or should not be playing for the national side. Once, joking about Jimmy Armfield's management style, Duncan McKenzie said that 'the manager's indecision is final', and now a similar hesitancy seemed to apply to Revie.

Throughout their careers, both Revie and Cocker had disapproved of footballers who seemingly lacked in dedication to their profession, and players who wanted to be 'rebels' rather than commit to teamwork and tactics. A player could have all the flair and talent in the world, but if he was lazy or lacking in fitness, and he wanted the rewards without grafting for them, then he wasn't good eno ugh for a Revie or Cocker team. English football possessed some wonderfully talented players, nowadays referred to as 'mavericks', but the England team needed more than just natural talent, they needed skilful workers too, who would never give in. Such players were few on the ground and Revie toiled, and was failing, to find a good-enough balance.

Football history was said to have been made at Bramall Lane, Sheffield, on 28 April 1977, with Laurie Cunningham selected for Les's under-21s side, becoming the first black footballer to play for England. Cunningham had only recently signed for John Giles's West Bromwich Albion from Leyton

Orient. The match was against Scotland, and England won 1-0 thanks to Cunningham's headed goal. Les said afterwards, 'I was extremely impressed with Cunningham's performance. He is clearly a very exciting player but his manager Johnny Giles wouldn't have paid £110,000 for him unless he thought he was going to make a tremendous impact in the game.'

What is certainly not a matter of historical record is the Football Association's prejudiced views at the time. When Harold Thompson learnt that Les had named three black players in his under-21 squad, he was not a happy misanthrope. He telephoned Les to express his disapproval at the decision, instructing that 'only one' black player would be 'allowed' to play in the match. Les, disgusted by Thompson's (and thus the FA's) bigotry, demanded the instruction be put in writing. The letter duly arrived, in the form of a memorandum, with the 'only one' comment reiterated, along with a written warning from Ted Croker that if Les talked to the press about 'England's selection process' then he would be in breach of contract. Viv Anderson was one of the three black players but it would be nearly a year before he made his debut. As things turned out, the under-21 fixture against Italy signified the first time of more than one black player representing England – Anderson and Cunningham in March 1978.

On Tuesday, 17 May 1977, at 3pm and at Hampden Park, a Glasgow XI played a Football League XI as part of the Queen's Silver Jubilee celebrations. Scotland boss Ally MacLeod managed the Glasgow team and Revie the Football

League group, with Les his assistant. The Scots won 2-1, while both teams wore horrendous kits, the colour schemes possibly even more jarring than artist Jamie Reid's work on Sex Pistols record covers. Leeds chairman Manny Cussins was in attendance and requested a quiet word with Les almost straight after the match. He wanted to offer Les the manager's job, even though Jimmy Armfield was still in charge at Elland Road. Les turned it down and later told Dave he had refused the job because the club was, politely speaking, 'in a mess', plus he did not trust the Leeds board.

As we have seen from earlier comments from Les himself, Leeds were not the only club to invite him to apply to be new manager, both Southampton and Tottenham Hotspur had expressed strong interest in acquiring his services. He turned Spurs down flat but the Saints role had been of interest, prompting him to travel with Nora down to Southampton to check things out. Les was impressed by the club and Nora loved the area but the Cocker family was already settled in Leeds, of course, and so the Southampton opportunity was declined.

By June 1977, Fourth Division Watford were in need of a new manager, having dismissed Mike Keen. Rock star Elton John had bought the club a year earlier and, according to Bobby Moore's wife Tina, had verbally offered the vacancy to the former England captain; they had even shaken hands on the deal. However, and unfortunately for Moore, Elton's choice was opposed by three of Watford's directors. Elton was in a quandary and so sought the opinion of Revie and Les; could they recommend anyone? In response, the duo questioned him on his ambitions for Watford – was he in it just for showbiz reasons or did he genuinely want to make them a good football club? It was the latter, he answered, and so Revie and Les recommended he speak with the young, ambitious, eager-to-learn manager named Graham Taylor, who they thought had the ability to really make things happen at one of the more 'unfashionable' clubs. A regular at England games and in the Esso Hotel suite afterwards, Taylor had already done a fine job at Lincoln City, winning the Fourth Division title the previous year with a record high number of points.

In the Home Internationals, having rather fortuitously defeated Northern Ireland 2-1 in Belfast, England hosted Wales at Wembley, played poorly and deservedly lost 1-0. In the Esso Hotel afterwards, Revie could hardly have felt more depressed, but somehow it happened, with the revelation from Ipswich manager Bobby Robson that he had been offered his job as England manager.

The following Saturday, 4 June, England lost 2-1 at home to Scotland. Les divulged ahead of the match that the England players had been working on defending set pieces, specifically to deal with the aerial threat of Gordon McQueen who Les and Revie knew virtually everything about. In coaching sessions, Joe Corrigan played in 'the McQueen role', with goalkeeper Ray Clemence and the England defenders instructed in how to play against McQueen until they were comfortable and clear on their responsibilities for the match. The big moment came in the 43rd minute when Scotland were awarded a free kick after a handball by Phil Neal near the left-hand edge of the penalty box.

Asa Hartford took the kick and chipped in a perfect cross to the area, where McQueen beat everyone to the ball to slam home a fine header to make it 1-0. After the game, Les remarked to son Dave, 'When we were at Leeds, we told the players what to do and they did it, simple as that, but some of this lot, they don't seem to have a clue.' McQueen, in a television interview, stated that the Scotland team had been working on set pieces too, and that whoever was taking the free kick was told to aim for the biggest thing on the pitch, which was his head.

At England's London hotel the morning after the Scotland defeat, Les gathered the squad together before they were set to embark from Heathrow on England's three-match tour of South America where they would play against Brazil, Argentina and Uruguay. Les advised the players that he would be in charge for the first match of the tour – the 8 June game against Brazil – because Revie had been given 'a bit of stick' of late so he had told the manager to have a rest for a few days before watching Finland against Italy in Helsinki. And so, while the England party flew to Rio de Janeiro, Revie would be travelling alone to Finland. It would, however, transpire much later that, having flown to Europe, the trip paid for by the FA, he had then bought another ticket to fly to the United

Arab Emirates. The news that he was not meant to know, from Robson, was prominent in his thoughts.

England ended up drawing 0-0 with Brazil, but had they been 3-0 up by half-time then no one could really have claimed an injustice, but eventually the heat, the humidity and the fatigue of long-distance travel began to affect the team. By the end, England were rather fortunate to have drawn. Clemence played brilliantly in goal and, on the rare occasion he was beaten, Trevor Cherry somehow intervened to make crucial blocks on the line. This had been a great spectacle to watch and a fine result for England and even the media enjoyed it, for the right reasons too, and the headline 'England Cocker Hoop!' appeared on back pages in England the following morning.

England's star player, Kevin Keegan, was also impressed, 'I thought Les Cocker did well, not droning on with a lot of detail but just saying, "Go out and enjoy it." We did enjoy it and we were really good for the first 20 minutes when we might have scored four. Les was a real old-time football man from the small clubs in the mid-50s. He was good, the perfect foil for Don Revie, and he surprised all of us when taking charge for our match in Brazil. He picked the team and was decisive about it, saying, "We'll play this way," and running through the tactics. For the first time I wondered if he might not have made a good number one somewhere. The league is full of Les Cockers, gnarled men who are steeped in football but never fulfil their maximum potential because they haven't got the chats. I noticed that with Les, he knew his stuff better than most modern coaches but could not put it over as clearly.'

Each to their own opinion but I think Les's stance on football management was less about 'having the chats' and more to do with not wanting to work with pompous and ignorant directors and chairmen.

John Motson was in Rio as commentator for BBC TV at the time. He was close to the England group and friends with future star Steve Coppell. They were out running together on the Copacabana Beach and, as Motson's training shoes were dirty, he asked physio Norman Medhurst if he could put them in with England's kit so as not to soil his own luggage for the next part of their tour journey. Medhurst agreed that it was fine but when Les Cocker found out, Les went on to give Motson a real dressing-down – it wasn't England's place to look after Motson's gear!

On Monday, 13 June, England drew 1-1 with Argentina. Trevor Cherry and Daniel Bertoni were sent off eight minutes from time. Cherry had appeared to jostle Bertoni and was promptly punched in the mouth by the Argentine, referee Ramón Barreto of Uruguay dismissing the pair. England had been greeted by cries of 'animals, animals' by the home crowd, a bitter reference to Alf Ramsey's remarks after the infamous 1966 World Cup encounter. Cherry, with blood streaming from his mouth as two front teeth had been knocked out, was led off the pitch and met abuse from the crowd throwing missiles at him and sunglasses-wearing Les.

Two days later came a 0-0 draw with Uruguay. Although it would be a few weeks before the news became public knowledge, this match would be Revie's last in charge of England. The match was a 'bore-draw', in which the hosts barely attacked while the visitors hardly had the energy to do so, it was the first time England had completed an unbeaten tour of South America.

On the flight back home, Revie told FA chairman Harold Thompson that he knew the FA planned to sack him and bring in Bobby Robson as his replacement. Revie was open to negotiating his departure but Thompson denied everything. As a result, Revie decided he would resign, once he had ensured security for himself. From what could be described as 'unwholesome', the situation was descending into an ugly scandal, brought on by the FA's lies and gross disrespect towards the England manager.

Back at Elland Road, Revie's secretary Jean Reid would be tasked with typing the letter of resignation and Les required to ensure it was delivered to the appropriate FA parties.

On 10 July 1977, Dave Cocker drove with his dad to the Sheffield home of Dick Wragg, the FA International Committee chairman, to hand deliver Revie's resignation. Les had also spoken by phone with Wragg, advising him that they would be delivering it. Copies of the letter had been posted to the FA headquarters at Lancaster Gate too. The following day, the *Daily Mail* printed a 'huge exclusive' revealing that Revie had quit as England manager. FA secretary Ted Croker would go on to claim that Revie's letter of resignation – one addressed to him and one to Thompson – hadn't been delivered until the day after the *Daily Mail* article appeared.

By late August 1977, Les had resigned as England's assistant manager. Revie's successor, Ron Greenwood, had asked Les to take charge of the under-21 side against Norway on 6 September. He gracefully declined the invitation.

11

The UAE and then 'Donny'

IN SEPTEMBER 1977, Les Cocker moved to Dubai to be assistant manager to Don Revie for the United Arab Emirates national team, contracted for two years. Their new employers wanted the duo to develop the team enough to be able to compete with 'all-conquering' Kuwait, and to effectively rebuild the sport on the firmest foundations possible.

Don and Elsie's son Duncan, interviewed in later years, said that the family had a great time in the Middle East, and that it was probably as happy as he'd seen his mum and dad. They were relaxed and they enjoyed the sunshine, they enjoyed the golf (both parents were avid golfers) and they enjoyed Dubai, making new friendships which remained strong until the end.

Kim Revie

Kim Revie was born to Elsie and Don in 1959 so she was accustomed to seeing much of Les while she was growing up. Les was often with her dad, as a colleague and as a close

10 March 1970: Don Revie with his son Duncan, daughter Kim and wife Elsie at Buckingham Palace after receiving the OBE.

friend. It would seem almost as if Les was an uncle to her and Duncan. I interviewed Kim in January 2022. 'Les was simply a lovely man. Decent, honest, caring, and a really close friend to my dad. Professionally, they complemented each other perfectly, an ideal partnership who relied on each other and trusted each other's judgement without fail. He had been integral in creating the family atmosphere at Elland Road while Dad was manager there, it was one of many principles and ideas that they agreed on in order to develop the football club into one of the best there was. I don't remember real details of their work together in the UAE, only that it seemed to be a huge amount of work to develop the team and the sport over there, almost as if they were starting from scratch as it all seemed very basic at the time, with hardly any solid framework or infrastructure in place.'

Although only a child at the time of her dad and Les's time at Leeds, Kim knows the history and how hard they worked to reinvigorate the club, advancing to achieve the astonishing success. 'Don and Les, and everyone else at the club, shared the principle that everyone should be united in working their hardest for the team, that teamwork and camaraderie were crucial in getting the best results. It genuinely was that old saying at Elland Road, 'side before self'. No matter how small a task was, it was worth completing as professionally as possible.' It is the approach that Kim has always tried to abide by. She is still in the music industry, working with various new young artists currently, having previously managed such names as Ali Campbell and UB40, Lynden David Hall, and Jamelia, among others.

In 1979, Don Revie said, 'Sir Harold Thompson, chairman of the FA, treated me like an employee. These Arab sheiks treat me like one of them.' It's an interesting comment, and he and Les and their families were invited to attend parties at the Royal Palace in Dubai. They weren't the only 'expats' out there of course, and Dave Cocker remembers a former Scotland Yard detective who had taken up a high-ranking role with Dubai's police force. The unnamed officer told the Revies and Cockers of his past career in London with Scotland Yard in the 1960s and 70s, and mentioned he had been part of the operation investigating the Kray twins, gathering evidence with a view to eventually arresting them – specifically in 1967, which happened to be the year when referee Ken Burns so controversially ended Leeds' FA Cup hopes in the semi-final against Chelsea at Villa Park, Birmingham. The Dubai-based officer revealed that he knew of, and had seen for himself, the ongoing observations of the Krays' nefarious activities, including photographs taken of their meeting referee Burns prior to the semi-final.

Rather than move out to Dubai, Dave and his wife Pauline stayed in Leeds with their young family. They managed to frequently visit his parents' Jumeirah villa, thanks in part to the generosity of his employers allowing him the time off. 'Dad only stayed two years, the duration of his contract,' said Dave, 'though Don stayed longer and went on to manage Al-Nasr. I think Dad was missing his golf as there was only one sand course in Dubai then! Mum didn't even want to go to the UAE at first, but she loved it out there and didn't want to come home really. We'd go over for a whole month at a time. Mum and Dad's house was set back about 500 metres from the beach.'

A wholly unacceptable note came when Bob Paisley's Liverpool team of 1978 were European champions and had been invited to play in a match to mark the opening of the new Al-Maktoum Stadium on 26 May 1978. However, due to Revie's association with the UAE, the English FA initially refused to authorise the game, such was their hatred of the man. They swiftly backed down after Liverpool confirmed the disgraceful, unacceptable situation to officials in Dubai who, in turn, promised the FA that the affair would be escalated and they would have a serious international and political scandal on their hands if they didn't co-operate

Doncaster Rovers

Les returned to England to work as assistant manager to Billy Bremner at Doncaster Rovers in the summer of 1979. He was working there voluntarily, being paid only for his travel expenses. It was probably a surprising move for many, but it made sense to Les even though Doncaster were in the Fourth Division as they were clearly ambitious, if not wealthy, and with Bremner at the helm the board really seemed to mean business.

Glynn Snodin

Glynn Snodin was born on 14 February 1960 and quite fittingly for that date he is the kind of person who wears his heart on his sleeve. His professional career commenced at Doncaster Rovers in 1977, and he would go on to make 309 appearances for the club, scoring 61 goals. From there he went to Sheffield Wednesday before joining Leeds in July 1987, clocking up 116 appearances and scoring 13 goals during a highly significant period for the club. Glynn is possibly (probably, I say) the inventor of the chest-thumping 'Leeds, Leeds, Leeds' salute. That might mean nothing to non-Leeds fans but, I assure you, it means plenty to the United's faithful. Anyway, I have been exceedingly lucky with the interviews for this book because they have all been fantastic to speak with, and Glynn was absolutely no exception, his South Yorkshire accent chiming with warmth and sincerity.

'I didn't know Les personally before he joined us at Doncaster Rovers,' he told me, 'but obviously I knew of him, me being a Leeds fan since 1972, and I knew his England work as well. I knew everything about Leeds and England in those days, every player, who was in the squad, even all the staff. In Billy Bremner, it was absolutely fantastic for me to have my favourite-ever player as my boss at Doncaster, and then he was joined by *the* Les Cocker. And they were a great pair together, they just bounced off each other, meaning that if Les saw Billy about to lose his temper over something minor, Les would pull him to one side and have a word in his ear, to calm things down. Like they were good cop, bad cop sort of, and it really worked. And we loved the Gaffer [Bremner], he was like a second dad and he always did what he thought was right for the team. We'd do anything for Billy, and Les was good for him as well, always ready to advise and share the benefit of his vast experience, sometimes just simple things like "Hang on a minute, let's look at it this way, from a different point of view." Yes, Les was great for the Gaffer.'

Did Les help Snodin with his own game? 'Yes. He used to go round everybody, to be honest, giving advice. We were a young side then and we definitely did need help. He'd ask us what we thought and then suggest doing different aspects of our game in a different way. He'd stay with you just helping you with your game, 15, 20 minutes. If you needed help, Les was always there for you. He'd tell you things but ask you things as well, he wanted your opinion, he wasn't just about ordering you about. He was fantastic, and what a real gentleman.

'I think, we all probably thought it, that Doncaster could have gone a real long way with Billy and Les together. We were a young side and we all thought they were the right pairing to get us where WE wanted to go. It was absolutely fantastic for us lads. I don't think anyone can talk bad about Les, I really don't think they can. To give an honest opinion on someone, you can only really go on how he is with yourself, and how he was with you, and I haven't a bad word to say about him. That's always what I go by, how he treats you and how he respects you. Every day was special to me when training with them two. It was just a pleasure to get up in a morning and go to work – you can't really call playing football "work"! To go into the football club knowing we were going to train under the Gaffer and Les Cocker. I mean, wow! What more do you need? Especially for me being a Leeds fan all my life, it was fantastic, I really loved it.'

Did Glynn take any of this into his own coaching or assistant manager career? If so then he must have been the 'good cop'? 'Well yes, most of the time but I have my moments! I just don't like losing if it's in a way where not everyone's tried their hardest, so some things do need saying to the players, but in an honest way. As long as you've given everything out on that pitch, then that's acceptable, every team's going to lose a match some time that they haven't deserved to. It's when a player throws the towel in, that's what we really don't like. As long as you keep going then we don't mind it but yes, if a player doesn't work hard then I can definitely lose it. I learnt from all those years back with Les. You learn every day in football. I'm still learning. I'm 61 and I'm still learning. You want to keep learning, I want to keep learning. I love listening to pundits, because nine out of ten times they do know what they're on about.'

As we know, Les was one of the main proponents of dossiers compiled on opposing teams and individual players. I asked Snodin if he used them at Doncaster. 'We didn't use dossiers as such at Doncaster but Les definitely did his homework and knew about opposing players. He'd have a word in your ear about such and such a player we'd be facing. He'd mention he was good at this and good at that, whether he liked to cut inside rather than run at you on the outside, whether they wanted the ball to feet or in behind the defender, and he'd know their strengths and weaknesses. He was very good at that and it was nice and helpful when you knew a bit about the opposition beforehand. Les was a great fella to have around the place. Always positive, jolly, upbeat, and him being like that made you feel better as well.'

I told Snodin that I couldn't help but think that the way he approached things and the decent manner with which he treated people came from what he had learnt and who he had learnt from or worked with. 'It is, yes. Me and my brother Ian were brought up from nothing really, grassroots and a council estate in a little miners' village and we both ended up playing in the top level of the game, which is great. And that's what we try to say to everybody – it can be done. No matter where you are, you don't need loads of money, if you've got a desire and a belief in life and you know what you want to do, you take your chance and you go for it. It's a matter of working hard. Yes, you're going to get knocked down sometimes but you get up and brush yourself down, learn from it and say, "Right, tomorrow's going to be a good day and we'll get on with it – I'll make sure I'll do better."' Glynn closed the interview by telling me that he expects to be shedding a few tears when he reads this book, because Les was such a lovely man.

Farewell, Les

Dave remembers he and his dad visiting Bill Taylor in hospital where he was in recovery from a brain haemorrhage. Within a few days, Les had died suddenly, of a heart attack, at just 55 years of age, after a training session with the Doncaster players. The date was 4 October 1979, the tragedy striking on one of the training fields.

To add to the already terrible situation, a certain official decided to make personal, grubby gain from the news, by disclosing information on the incident to the local media before even Les's loved ones had been advised. This was all disgusting, disgraceful behaviour on these grimy individuals' part and profoundly upsetting to Les's family and friends, of course. I have learned how painful it is to this day for the Cocker family and I can't quite imagine the stress and tension it caused at the time. It has genuinely been a difficult matter to ask and write about. Dave Cocker explained to me that he had been at work when he received instruction to go to his parents' home, without explanation as to why. 'By the time I got there, Don Revie and Jack Charlton telephoned me but they both hung up quickly as it was obvious I didn't know anything about what had happened. No one had personally told them the news, they'd heard it before us via the media. Billy Bremner collected my brother Stephen from his NCB pit job near Doncaster to tell him. Billy then set off to Leeds with Stephen to see myself and Mum. He had telephoned my work and left a message with the receptionist to contact me for him to meet him at Mum and Dad's house. When I got the message I initially thought it would be to go for a game of golf that afternoon. In his car, while Billy was driving up to

THE UAE AND THEN 'DONNY'

Leeds with Stephen, they heard it announced on Radio 2. By the time they arrived, I had already realised something serious had happened due to so many hung-up calls. And when they arrived, just by looking at Billy and Stephen's faces, I knew exactly. The next step for me was to find out where Mum and my brother Ian were, as soon as possible, so that we could tell them first-hand. We finally found Mum doing her voluntary work cleaning at Lower Wortley Methodist Church. I told her about Dad and she asked if it had been a car accident, I said no it had been a heart attack in training. She said, "Bloody football", and she always blamed Dad's workload for it. We took her home and I then drove to Ian's house in Pudsey but there was no one in there and it was a while before we tracked him down. Billy was livid that the news had already broken as he had informed the police and arranged for all the Doncaster players to be kept in Rovers supporters club next to Belle Vue ground, so as to keeo it all quiet until we the family had been told. A police sergeant was posted on the door. It was him who rang Radio Hallam to reveal the news and get paid for it, probably around £20, then Hallam sold the news on. They didn't bloody care about my dad or us! I phoned Millgarth Police Station in Leeds to ask if they could help trace Ian's car as he will have been driving and I didn't want him driving and then hearing it on the radio. The police in Leeds were gob-smacked when I told them what happened.'

Dave went on to tell me that Bremner arranged for all the South Yorkshire football clubs to boycott Radio Hallam and ban them from covering their matches until they named the source. Apparently they did so, complete with an apology for their actions. Dave said, 'I phoned back to Dubai later that day, we could both hardly speak. I told Don not to bother flying home as there was nothing he could do, and I also spoke to Duncan and he travelled to Leeds to see us the next day with Billy.'

Glynn Snodin was in the changing rooms at Belle Vue with the other Doncaster players when Bremner told them that something had happened to Les. The players were asked to wait in the supporters' club. 'We couldn't work out what was happening, it was all a blur, really. When we were told that Les had died, we were all in a trance just about, in disbelief. Just a truly awful, awful day. Billy asked us to stay there while he tried to sort things out; I'm not sure whether he was fully aware of what had happened yet either, but he wanted to make sure that word didn't get out from us as things like that need to be dealt with correctly, don't they? That's what Billy was doing, the right thing, thinking about others. We were all devastated.'

Epilogue

ON 10 June 2009, members of England's 1966 World Cup-winning squad were presented with their winners' medals by prime minister Gordon Brown at a reception in Downing Street. When England lifted the World Cup it was customary then for only the 11 players on the pitch at the final whistle to be awarded the medals. Forty-three years later, FIFA had decided to award medals to every winning squad player from 1930 to 1974, plus the managers and their staff. George Cohen collected a medal on behalf of the family of Sir Alf Ramsey.

The players awarded their medal were Peter Bonetti, Ron Springett, Jimmy Armfield, Gerry Byrne, Ron Flowers, Norman Hunter, Terry Paine, Ian Callaghan, John Connelly, George Eastham and Jimmy Greaves. David Cocker accepted a medal on behalf of Les, and Margaret Shepherdson received a medal on behalf of her husband, Harold Shepherdson. The players and their families later left Downing Street and boarded an England team coach to take them to Wembley where they were due to be presented on the pitch before the England v Andorra World Cup qualifying match.

Dave took son Lee as his guest for the day. Attendees had to pay their own way there, so George Eastham had to fly in from South Africa at his own expense, for instance. Dave remembers a tube strike that day so road traffic was much heavier, more a case of organised chaos. The coach from Downing Street was making slow progress and had only police outriders rather than a full official escort. The driver had a word with one of the outriders who in turn contacted Downing Street to request an escort. Soon there were police motorbikes all around and the road opened up, and Hunter told Dave, 'It's just like old times, Dave!'

The on-pitch presentation was originally planned for before the match kicked off but the coach arrived too late, so it would take place during the half-time interval. And so, while the England and Andorra players walked back to the dressing rooms with the score 3-0 to England, the 1966 entourage was led on to the pitch. Whether the current players ignored them or didn't realise who they were was not clear, but only England boss Capello and player Steven Gerrard actually acknowledged them. Dave recalled that David Beckham walked past Lee Cocker and Lee said something to him that 'wasn't very nice'. Gerrard went to Gerry Byrne, the former Liverpool full-back, and hugged him. Jimmy Greaves was interviewed while on the pitch and criticised the Andorra players' performance saying that the 1966 lads could beat them. After the match in the stadium stands, Dave also remembers, when the 1966 party were in one of the FA's private and very plush bars, FA officials freely 'obtaining' bottles of spirits from behind the bar to take back to their hotel rooms for later.

In November 2009, Dave travelled by rail down to London with Dr Ian Adams and Ray Wilson. 'I took Doc as my guest to Alf Ramsey's statue/bust unveiling at Wembley in 2010 with the 1966 World Cup squad. This was the last time I saw Doc Phillips who was also there. No one seems to have any idea where Alf's statue is now, it seems to be a mystery.'

The Guardian commented on the unveiling, 'The bronze bust will be situated in the players' tunnel at Wembley and, in the words of George Cohen, vice-captain of the 1966 team who unveiled it with Fabio Capello, "It will remind every player to give their best out on the pitch." Players from the 1966-winning team, including the hat-trick scorer Geoff Hurst, Bobby Charlton, Ray Wilson, Martin Peters and goalkeeper Gordon Banks were at Wembley.'

Nora Cocker's pension – bearing in mind that Les had paid the pension scheme from 1946 to 1977, the year of his last paid job in England – had risen to the princely sum of £10.79 a week by the time she died, aged 94, in 2019. To use that annoying American-English phrase, '*You* do the math.' Someone had been ripping off the players' Football League pension scheme, but thankfully Mick Bates and Rod Belfitt formed a partnership to set up private financial arrangements for footballers after Dave had met the Leeds players and told of his mum's widows' pension after Les died in 1979. Similar suspicious stuff had clearly been occurring with his

FA pension as well, which had reached the heady heights of £2.79 per week (after 16 years of service to the FA from 1961 to 1977) in 2019.

Acknowledgements and Thanks

So much goodwill and generosity has been shown for Les Cocker in the making of this book. Of course, my biggest thanks go to Dave Cocker and Pauline, Lee and the rest of Les's family, and Ian Thornton has been a huge help, as is his wont – scragends are we!

Thanks and appreciation to:

Keith Annal
Chris and Adele Archer
Rob Bagchi
Gavin Blackwell
Aidan Butterworth
Jim Cadman
Mark Campbell
Colin Carmichael
Paul Cave
Allan Clarke
George and Daphne Cohen
Nigel Davey

Damian Dexter

Gary Edwards

Norma Emery

Samantha Emery and Sophie Cater Emery

Gerry and Anna Francis

Tracey Ford

Richard Gardham

John Giles

Eddie Gray

Louisa Harris

Phil Hay

Zoe Hinchliffe

Paul Jobson

Claire and Andrew Knowles

Peter Leatham and Accrington Stanley Supporters' Club

Tony Levison

Jim Lister

David Lloyd

Willie McInnes

Chris Miller

Mike O'Grady

Adam Pope

Nick Quantrill

Kim Revie

Steve Rhodes, researcher extraordinaire

Paul Robinson

Thom Roe

ACKNOWLEDGEMENTS AND THANKS

Mark Rutter
Tony Sealey
Gareth Senior
Glynn Snodin
John Stiles
Gordon Taylor
Ian Thornton
Paul Trevillion
Ian Watts

Bibliography

Books

Bagchi, Ro., *The Biography of Leeds United* (Vision Sports Publishing, 2020)

Ball, A., *Playing Extra Time* (Macmillan UK, 2009)

Bowler, D., *Winning Isn't Everything: A Biography of Sir Alf Ramsey* (Orion, 2013)

Brooking, T., *My Life in Football: Trevor Brooking* (Simon & Schuster, 2014)

Clayton, D., *Big Joe – the Joe Corrigan Story* (Fort Publishing, 2008)

Cohen, G., *My Autobiography* (Greenwater Publishing, 2003)

Cope, Q., and Collins, S., *Tony Collins: Football Master Spy* (Book Guild Publishing, 2012)

Croker, T., *The First Voice You Will Hear Is* (Collins, 1987)

Davies, H., *The Glory Game* (Mainstream Publishing, 2000)

Edwards, G., *No Glossing Over It* (Mainstream Publishing, 2013)

Endeacott, R., and Varley, A., *Leeds United: A Celebration – the Official Centenary Book* (ACA Creative Limited, 2019)

Endeacott, R., *Disrepute – Revie's England* (Tonto Books, 2010)

Giles, J., *John Giles: A Football Man – My Autobiography* (Hodder & Stoughton, 2010)

Glanville, B., *The Story of the World Cup* (Faber and Faber, various editions)

Gray, E., *Marching on Together* (Hodder & Stoughton, 2001)

Hardaker, A., and Butler, B., *Hardaker of the League* (Pelham Books, 1977)

Harrison, P., *The Black Flash: the Albert Johanneson Story* (Vertical Editions, 2012)

Hunter, N., *Biting Talk, My Autobiography* (Hodder & Stoughton, 2004)

Hurst, G., *Geoff Hurst: My Autobiography – 1966 And All That* (Headline Book Publishing, 2001)

Jackman, M., *Accrington Stanley, a Complete Record, 1894–1962* (Breedon, 1991)

James, G., *Joe Mercer, OBE: Football with a Smile* (James Ward, 2012)

Jarred, M., and Macdonald, M., *Leeds United: A Complete Record* (Breedon, 1996)

Keegan, K., *Against the World: Playing for England* (Sidgwick & Jackson, 1979)

Leeds United Official Handbook 1963/64 (Leeds United Football Club, 1963)

Lorimer, P., and Rostron, P., *Peter Lorimer: Leeds and Scotland Hero* (Mainstream Publishing, 2002)

McKinstry, L., *Jack and Bobby: A Story of Brothers in Conflict* (Willow, 2005)

McKinstry, L., *Sir Alf* (HarperSport, 2006)

Motson, J., *Motty* (Virgin Books, 2009)

Phillips, Dr N., *Doctor to the World Champions: My Autobiography* (Trafford, 2009)

Revie, D., *Leeds United Book of Football* (Souvenir Press, 1969)

Revie, D., *Leeds United Book of Football 2* (Souvenir Press, 1970)

Rowlinson, J., *Boys of 66* (Virgin Books, 2016)

Ruppert, J., *World Cup Cortinas* (Foresight Publications, 2014)

Shaw, P., *The Book of Football Quotations* (Mainstream Publishing, 1999)

Thompson, P., *Stand Up Pinocchio* (Trinity Mirror Sport Media, 2008)

Trevillion, P., and Jeffries, N., *The Beaver: A Story of Sock Tags and Self Belief* (Scratching Shed Publishing, 2022)

Tyler, M., The Boys of '66 (Hamlyn Publishing, 1981)

Newspapers

Aberdeen Evening Express

Belfast Telegraph

Birmingham Daily Post

Coventry Evening Telegraph

Daily Mirror

Football Post

Hull Daily Mail

Liverpool Echo

Newcastle Evening Chronicle

Newcastle Journal

Nottingham Evening Post

Sports Argus

Star Green 'Un

Stockport Advertiser

The Gardian

Yorkshire Post and Evening Post

Websites

www.11v11.com
www.britishnewspaperarchive.co.uk
www.comedy.co.uk
www.englandfootballonline.com
www.englandstats.com
www.gameofthepeople.com

BIBLIOGRAPHY

www.gerryco23.wordpress.com
www.gogogocounty.org
www.historic-uk.com
www.iwm.org.uk
www.leeds-fans.org.uk
www.lfchistory.net
www.massobservation.amdigital.co.uk
www.mfc.co.uk
www.mightyleeds.co.uk
www.montagucup.com
www.nationalfootballmuseum.com
www.nonleaguematters.co.uk
www.oakwoodchurch.info
www.ozwhitelufc.net.au
www.peteranthony.co.uk
www.rcpe.ac.uk
www.silkmenarchives.org.uk
www.sport360.com
www.staceywest.net
www.stats.football.co.uk
www.strawberrynorth.co.uk
www.teesvalleyweb.com
www.thecelticwiki.com
www.theguardian.com
www.tynecastlefc.co.uk
www.varietygolf.org.uk
www.wsc.co.uk
www.yorkshirepost.co.uk